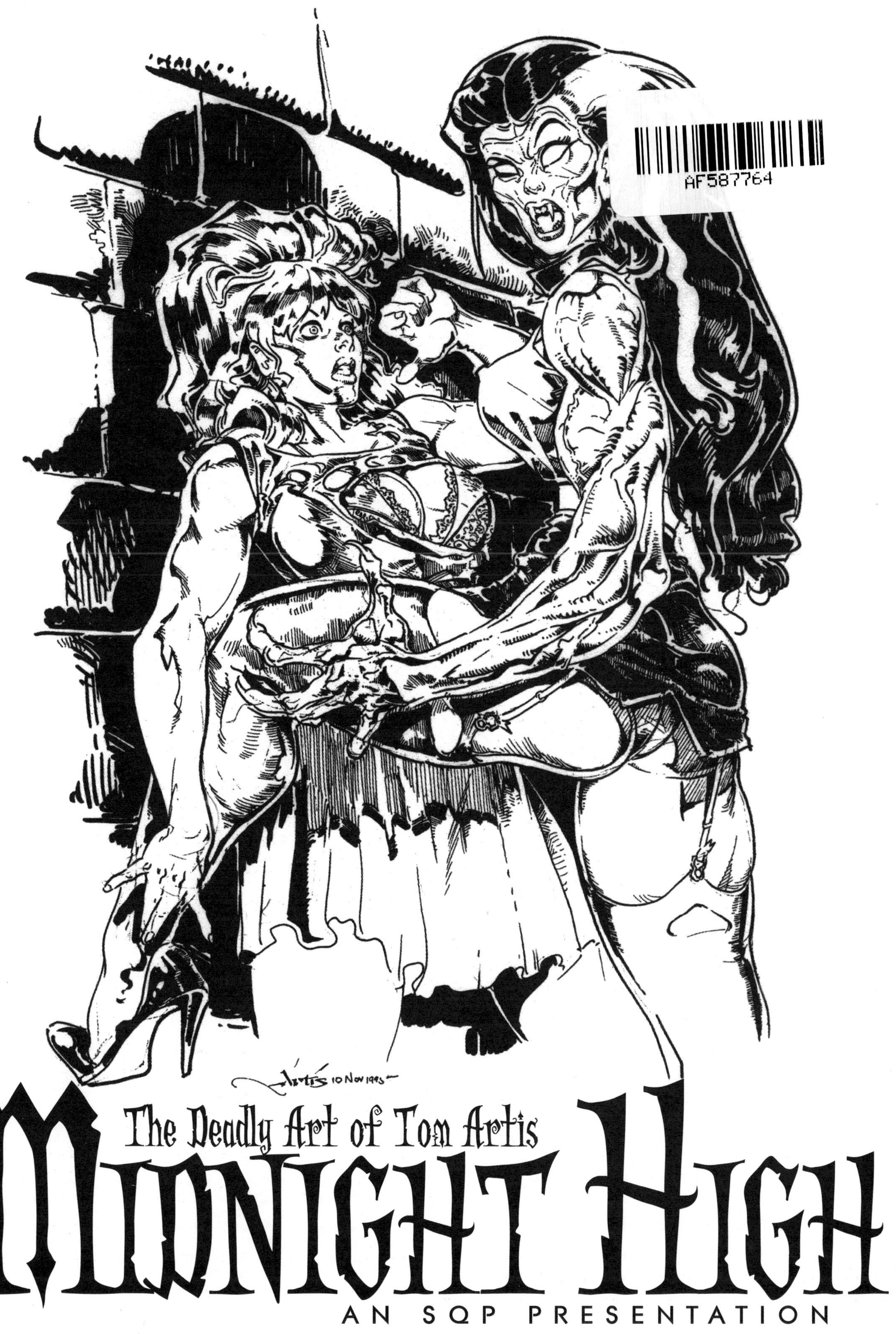
The Deadly Art of Tom Artis
MIDNIGHT HIGH
AN SQP PRESENTATION

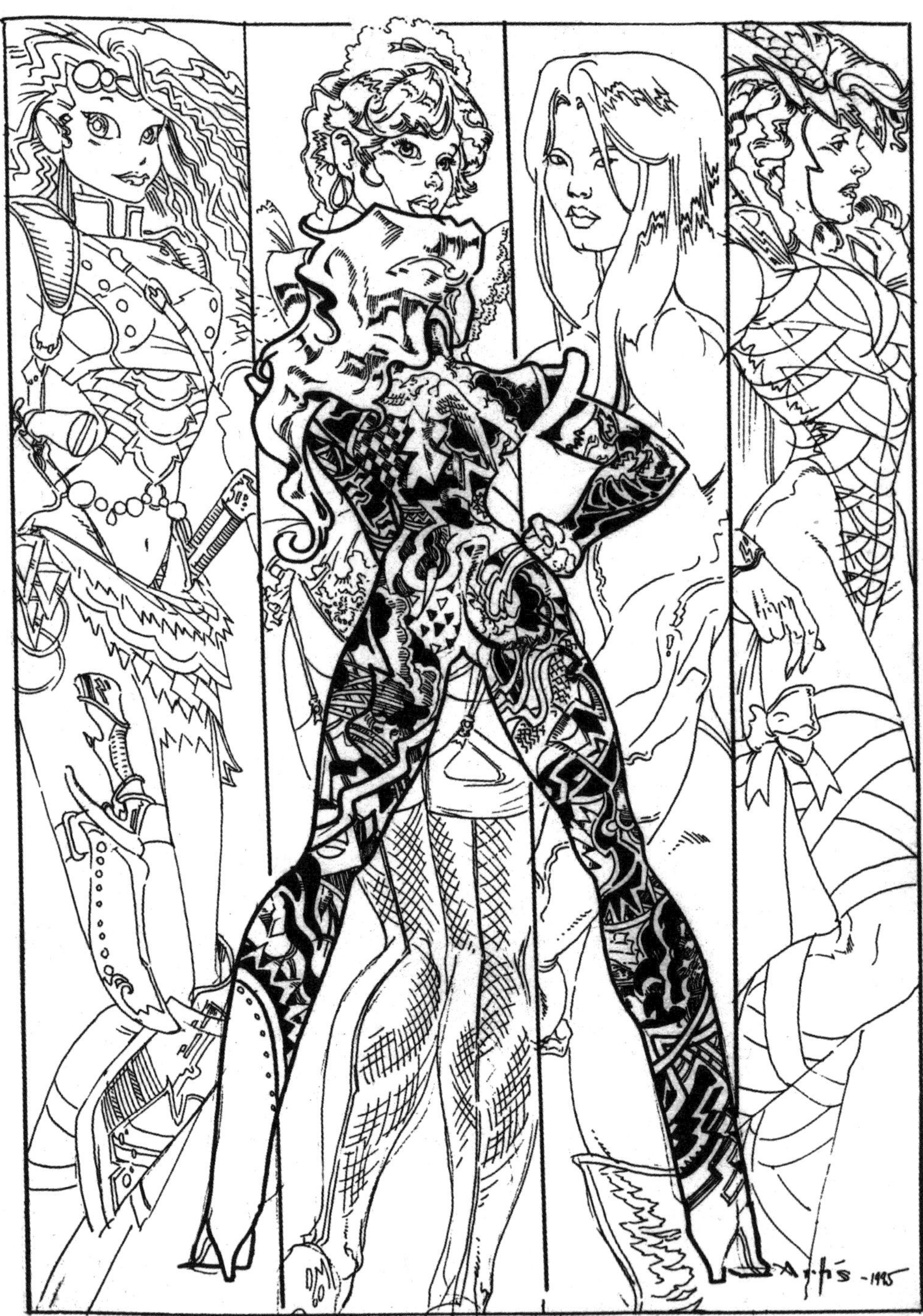

MIDNIGHT HIGH

The Deadly Art of Tom Artis

Book design by Grassy Knoll Studios.
Publishers: Sal Quartuccio and Bob Keenan

SQP Inc.
PO Box 550 - Howell, NJ 07731

Midnight High: a letter from the Principal

And this begins the part where I'm supposed to tell you (the reader) something about myself- so I suppose I'll start with the most commonly asked questions...

How did you get into the business and whatever happed to you?

I've been drawing pictures since I was about two years old (admittedly, badly..)and about age three or four some educational type told my parents that I displayed abilities beyond the normal level of other kids my age. After reading up on the histories of the Old Masters, I decided that being an artist was the most interesting thing I'd ever heard about being...and despite the stories of their tragic lives, it was a challenge only the most exceptional people took up...sort of like the best of an ascetic life and being an explorer - and getting paid for it. (As you may have deduced...I was a creepy little kid.)

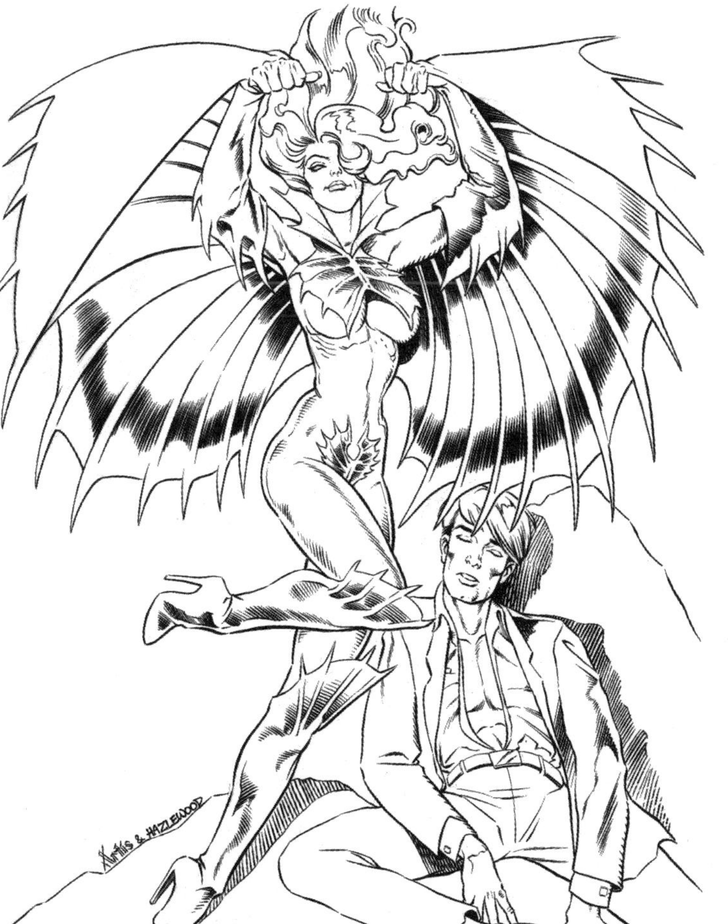

More importantly, it was something I could do by myself, without expensive training or specialized tools or complex degrees.

I grew up alone, and was encouraged to be self-reliant. Mind you, I wasn't lonely, but I was just so amazed by the things I saw and experienced, I spent most of my time in a daze of dreams and discovery.

Interacting with people, by comparison, was sharp and brilliant, with lots of jagged edges, and brutal, cruel interfaces, so I spent most of my time observing the complexities and confusing behavior of adults.

I grew up introspective, distant and obsessed with the idea of making myself strong and powerful. Being a young African-American child in the '50's, I was acutely aware of the threats all around me. I watched the Civil Rights Movement unfold around me courtesy of the First Source - the television. I was awed by the exploding Space Program and the Mercury Seven Astronauts...and, of course there were the comics...

Maybe I'm the product of the '60's culture, but I grew up believing in the old-fashioned Boy Scout, comic book, Truth, Justice, and the American way stuff. And even though I'm an old guy now, and I've been exposed to the cruelty and complexity of the modern world, I still believe in that strange old ethical stuff.

When I was little, my mother brought home comics (she worked nights at the hospital). I didn't know who Carl Barks was, but I read those Duck comics and the Harvey stuff like gospel - which, I suppose they were. When I was about five or six, I read my first Batman comic, and even though it was the rankest fantasy, I loved that stuff - and still do.

Now, even at five, I didn't really believe in the idea that a man in his underwear drives around in a supercar whipping armed men, but I found the idea of a person who had, through dedication and practice, achieved nearly super-human performance, appealing.

That lead me down the primrose path into adventure stories, and I systematically devoured everything I could read, from Asimov to Zahn, always searching out the great stories and the great heroes...and along the way, the great monsters.

Around the age of eight, I read a "How to Draw" book by a guy named Dave Breger, a moderately successful cartoonist. He posited doing a hundred drawings a day as the way to acquire facility and speed. that regimen I adopted, and armed with a cheap K-Mart Scribble Pad and Bic Accountant Five-Point pen, I began - and continued for nearly twenty years.

I found some amazing writers and artists along the way. I encountered E.E. Doc Smith in Junior High, then Cordwainer Smith, J.G. Ballard, Howard Fleming, Brand, Gibson, E.R. Eddison and Tolkien, all in High School. By then I was into detective fiction, and I read every one I could find.

In the comics, I discovered all the American greats and a few of the European ones. I read Tintin by Herge, Peyo's Smurfs, Asterix and Obleix by Goscinny and Uderzo.

I tracked Gil Kane back through Burne Hogarth to Paul Hogarth, Norman Rockwell and Rockwell kent and '60's designer Bob Peak.

I studied calligraphy. Japanese printmakers (particularly Hokusai) typography - I was all over the place, trying to define and collate all this data in to manageable forms. Someday maybe I'll write a little book on some of the stuff I learned in the strange mental meanderings I encountered.

By the time I hit college I had met some truly brilliant local artists who introduced me to a whole new universe of the arts.

Tim Conrad, who I informally apprenticed under, and Chuck Baxter, sign painter-engineer-ex-pro wrestler, taught me about the skills and strategies of the artists, both in business and day to day life.

I entered the comics industry pretty well-read, optimistic, fresh-faced, full of dreams and visions. Boy, was I stupid.

I got hired by First, then Marvel and then DC within about a year, and settled down to what I hoped would be a long, moderately-successful career and hit the brilliant sharp-edged, competitive world of comics in the early '90's when the fecal material horizontally intersected with the oscillating atmospheric recycler.

I thought, foolishly, that the key to success was brilliant draftsmanship and strong imaginative design. I didn't understand the ongoing battle between talent and executives.

I did this strip for DC called "Tailgunner Jo". I did around four pages a day and detailed the hell out of everything. The comic book - admittedly weird in concept - called for cartooning, futuristic designs, epic storytelling - the big showcase, right?

Somebody in editorial decided that a Japanese Manga style was called for. The resulting finished art was inked by a fine illustrator with a strong, personal style, who stripped my pencils down, dropped out the textures, and generally mutilated the job. I was deeply embittered, but resolved to be a professional about it.

It never got any better. I was told my inks were inferior, my covers were insipid, my drawings were sloppy and childish, you name it. They probably were, and I spent the remainder of my time in comics trying to meet their standards, which I never seemed to be able to do. I submitted proposals - all rejected.

I tried changing styles to no avail.

The mini-series I worked on - although they sold well, never seemed to appeal to the larger audience.

I developed a reputation as a troublesome, angry hack of limited ability.

I've never really understood why I took such a pasting...still don't understand to this day.

I'm still pretty sore about my comics experiences, but I did get to meet and work with some brilliant creative and editorial people, including legends like Dick Giordano, P. Craig Russell, Joe Rubinstein, Al Vey, Doug Moench, Peter Gillis, Doug Rice, Mike Parobeck, Howard Chaykin, Neal Adams, Todd Cameron Hamilton, and Sal Quartuccio.

And so, like a defeated prospector who had missed out on staking a claim in a gold rush, I staggered back to Springfield, Il. I have to say, the comics were a lot of fun, and a great adventure, but having turned that page, it was time to move on to other things.

Probably as a after-effect of the stresses I undertook, it took a while to re-establish my personal relationship with the muse. I rediscovered the fun of drawing, freed of deadline pressure and the trauma of competition...found a wife, started a family, settle down to a quiet sort of retirement, and died.

Actually, it was a nine-day diabetic coma which left me debilitated and obese (330 lbs), but that was close enough for me.

That was about three or four years ago, and in this "new" life, I'm a much different person. I'm back into martial arts for the first time in ten or fifteen years - strict dieting and lot of housework for exercise, including four of the most charming, obstreperous kids you could shake a stick at, blended family and all.

I lost some of the weight (last check, 254), healed some of the damage, and I'm back in training for Round Two. Like any fighter, the only person I ever have to beat is myself.

My goals:
To establish a new school of narrative art by really exploring how comics work. You realize that both the comics medium and the animation industry were created by the actions of one person - Winsor McCay (Little Nemo).

This is a truly stunning intellectual achievement which cannot by overstated. this sort of achievement in the modern world is equalled only by people like Nikola Tesla who created both AC power and broadcast (wireless) transmission.

To explore new mediums, new technologies, new approaches - trying out new art - areas like hand-painting motorcycle tanks, multi-media projects with organics, sculptural forms, and my greatest new achievement - harassing small children into doing homework.

-Tom Artis

The character Carbide, (Drill-sergeant's hat)is a exiled superhero form the domed world, who retire to this desert world, and acts as its marsha Here he's guarding a carava

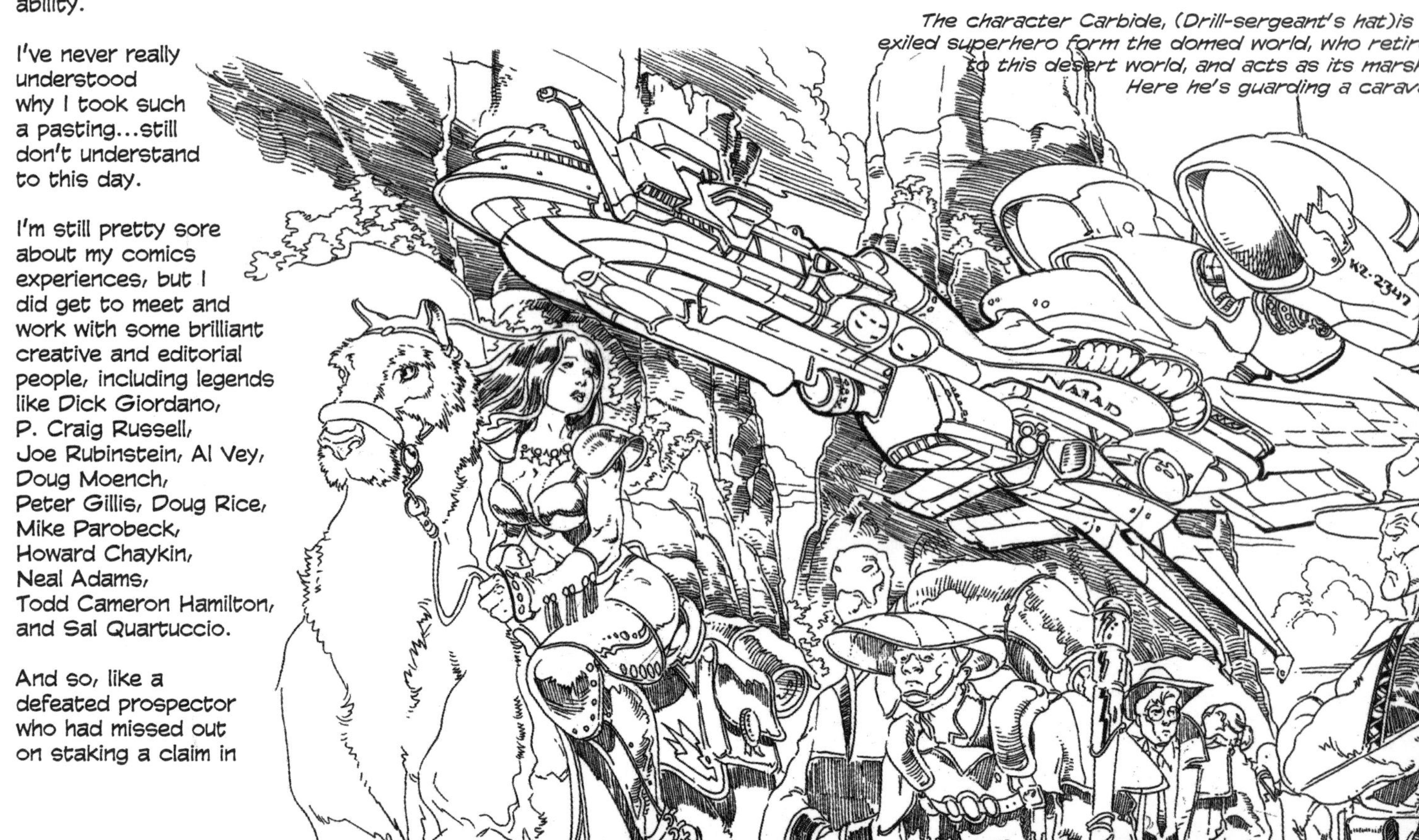

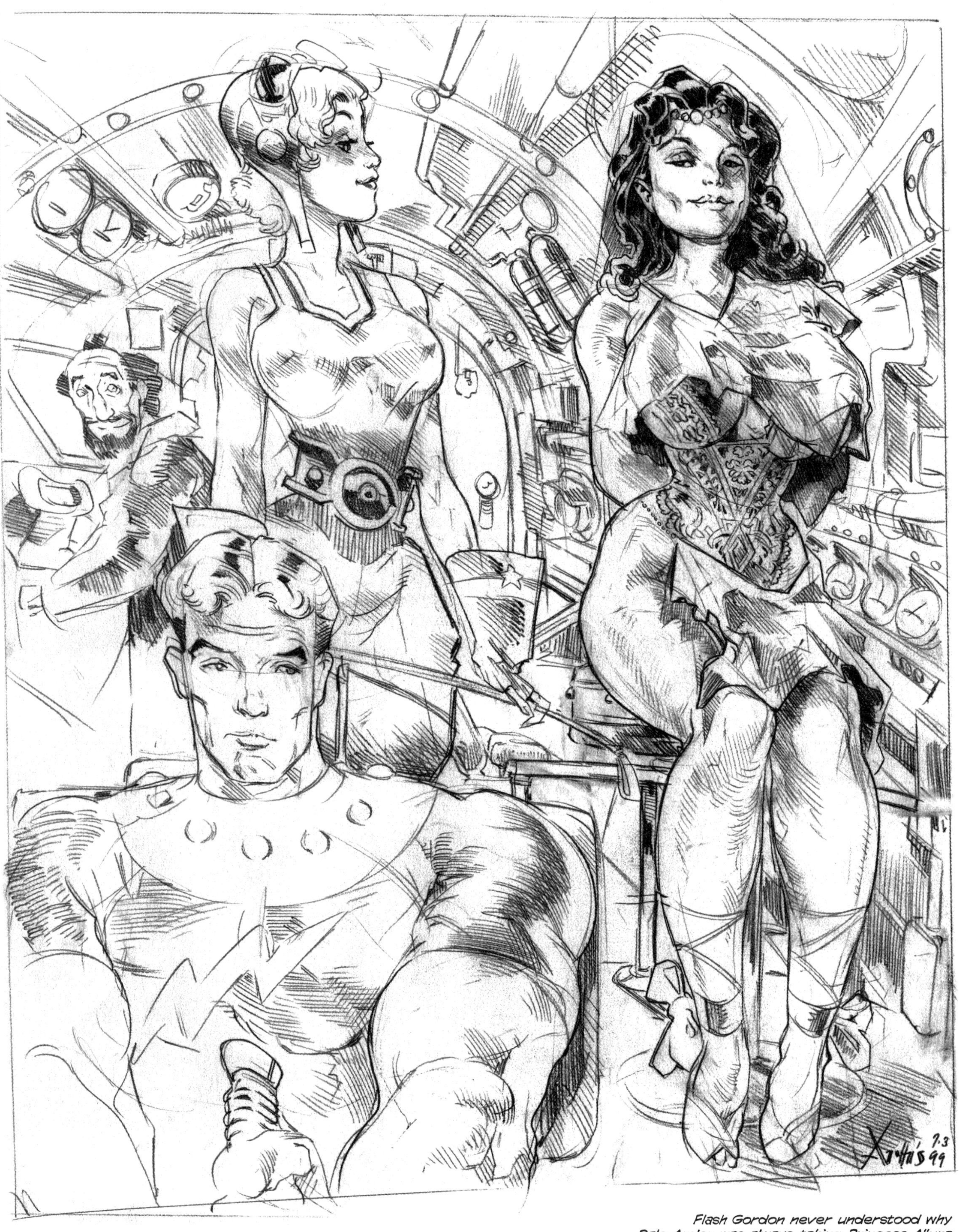

Flash Gordon never understood why Dale Arden was always taking Princess Allura back to Ming's castle to "further her education"

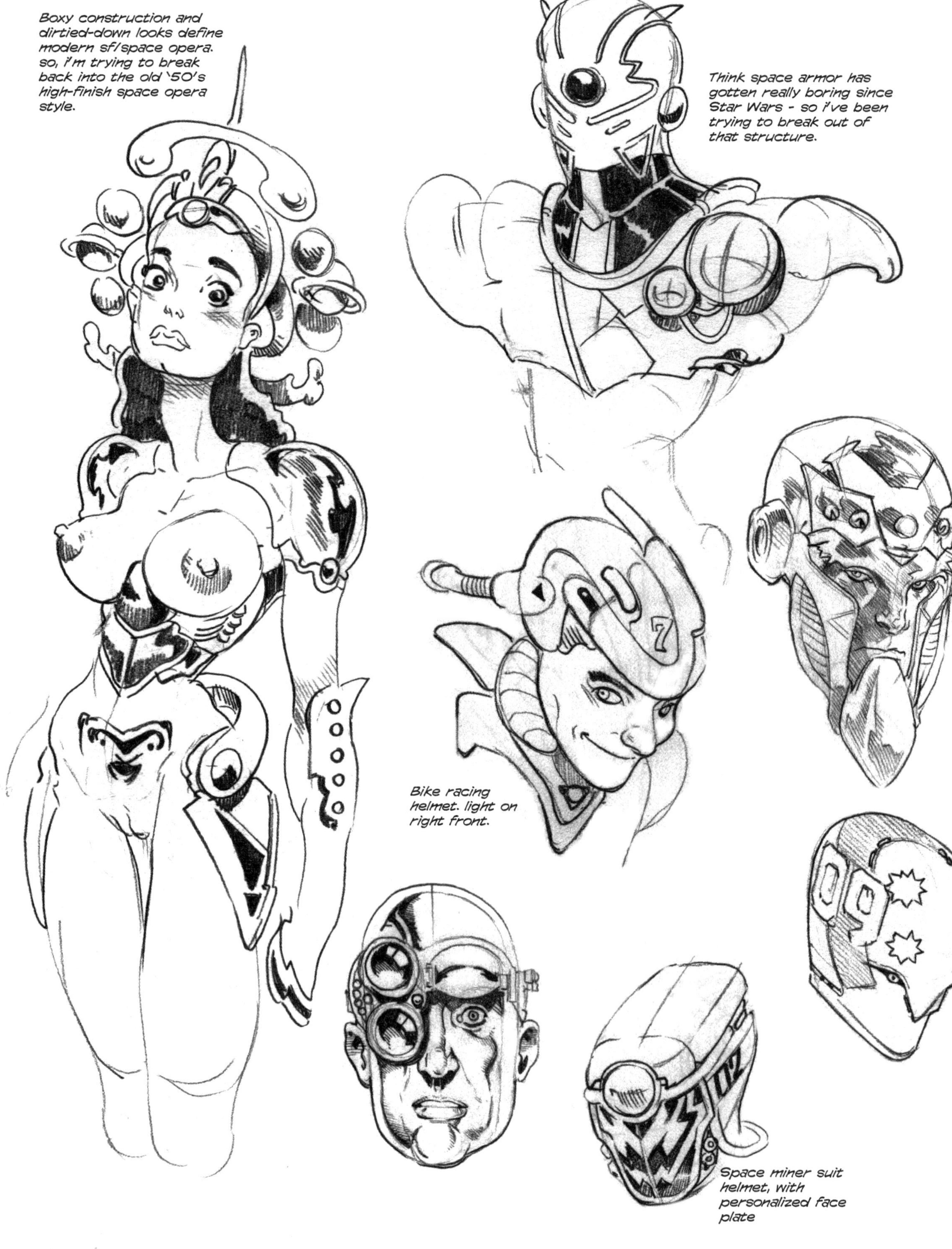
Boxy construction and dirtied-down looks define modern sf/space opera. so, i'm trying to break back into the old '50's high-finish space opera style.
Think space armor has gotten really boring since Star Wars - so i've been trying to break out of that structure.
7
Bike racing helmet. light on right front.
02
Space miner suit helmet, with personalized face plate

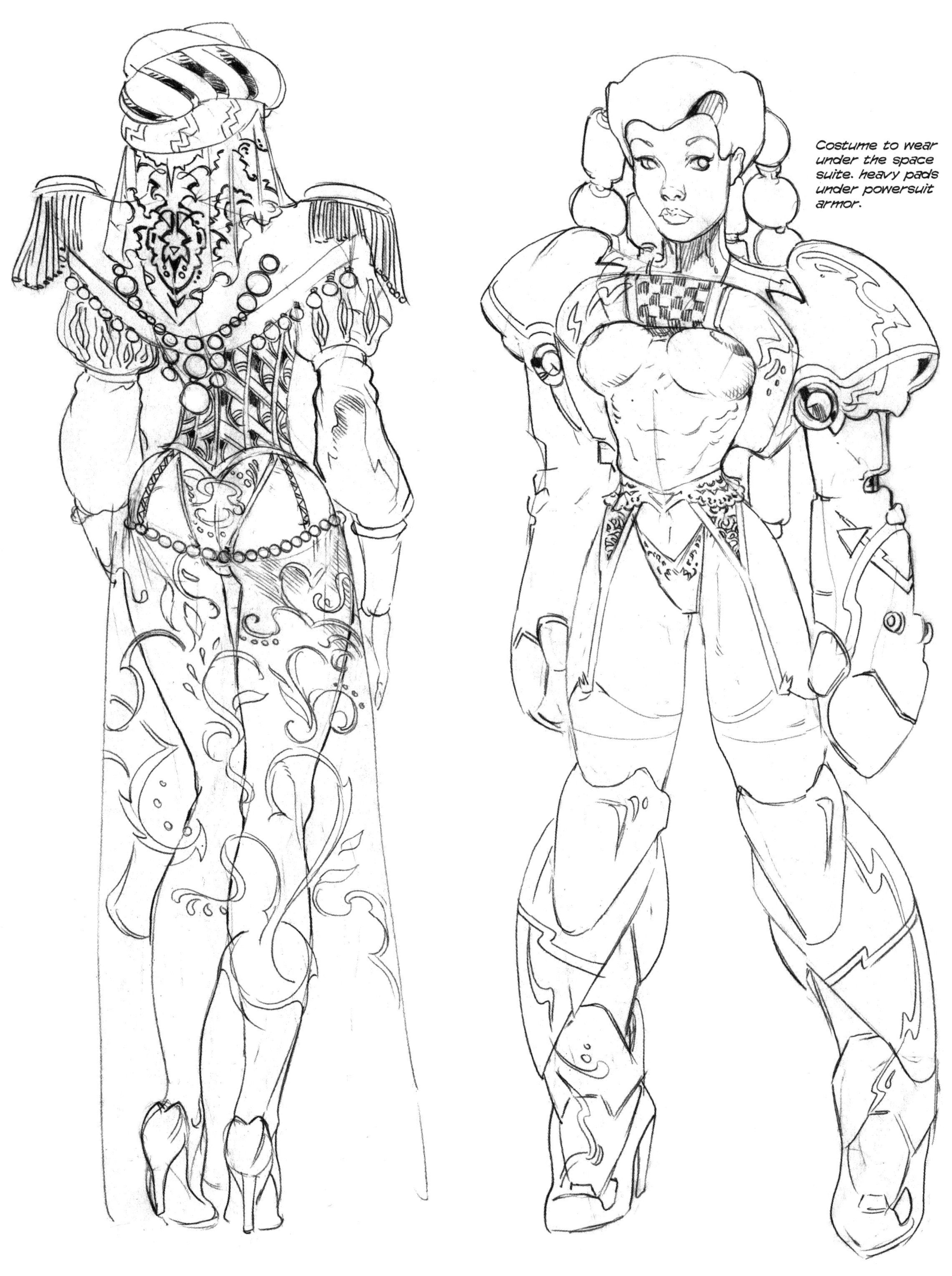
Costume to wear
under the space
suite. heavy pads
under powersuit
armor.

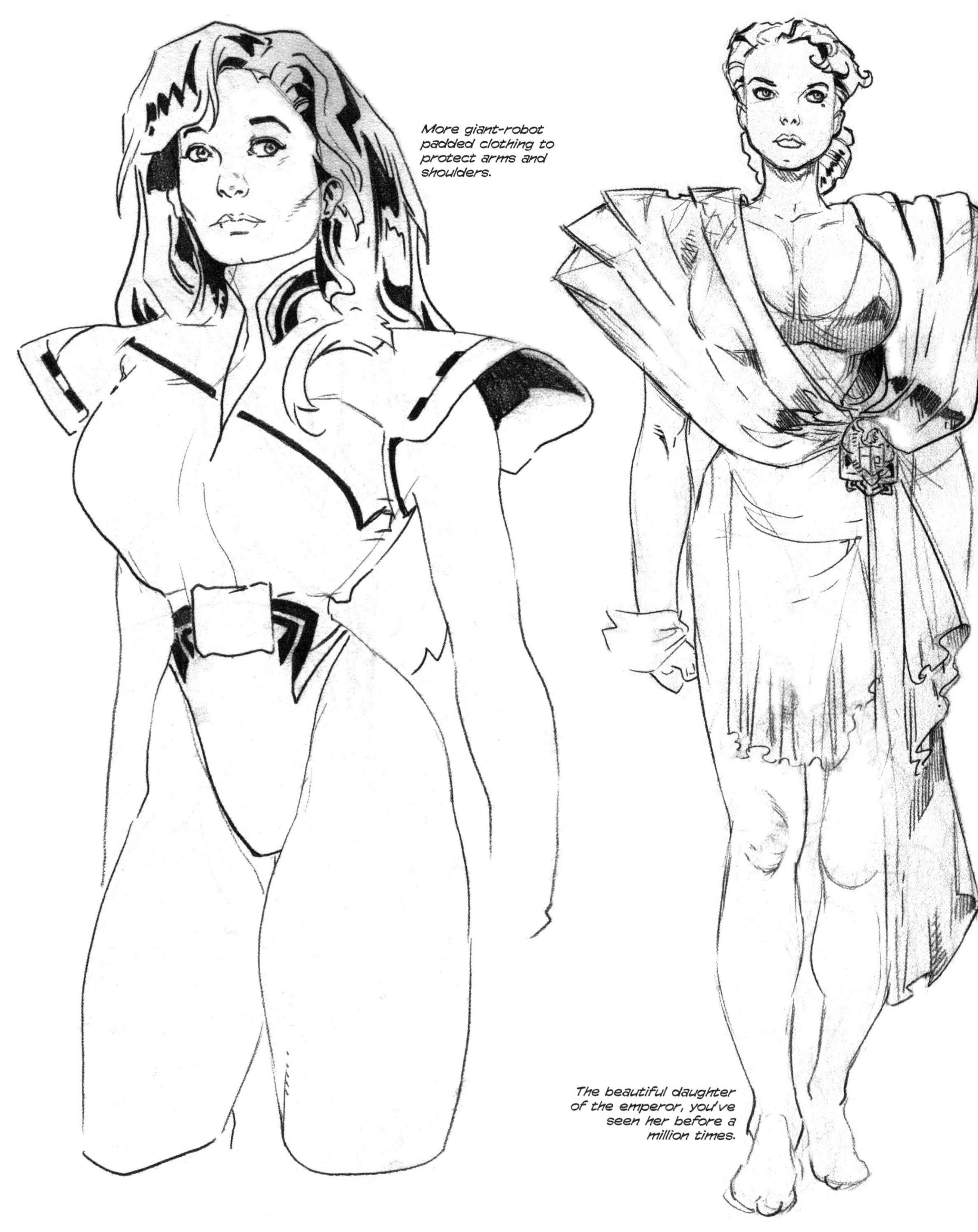
More giant-robot
padded clothing to
protect arms and
shoulders.
The beautiful daughter
of the emperor, you've
seen her before a
million times.

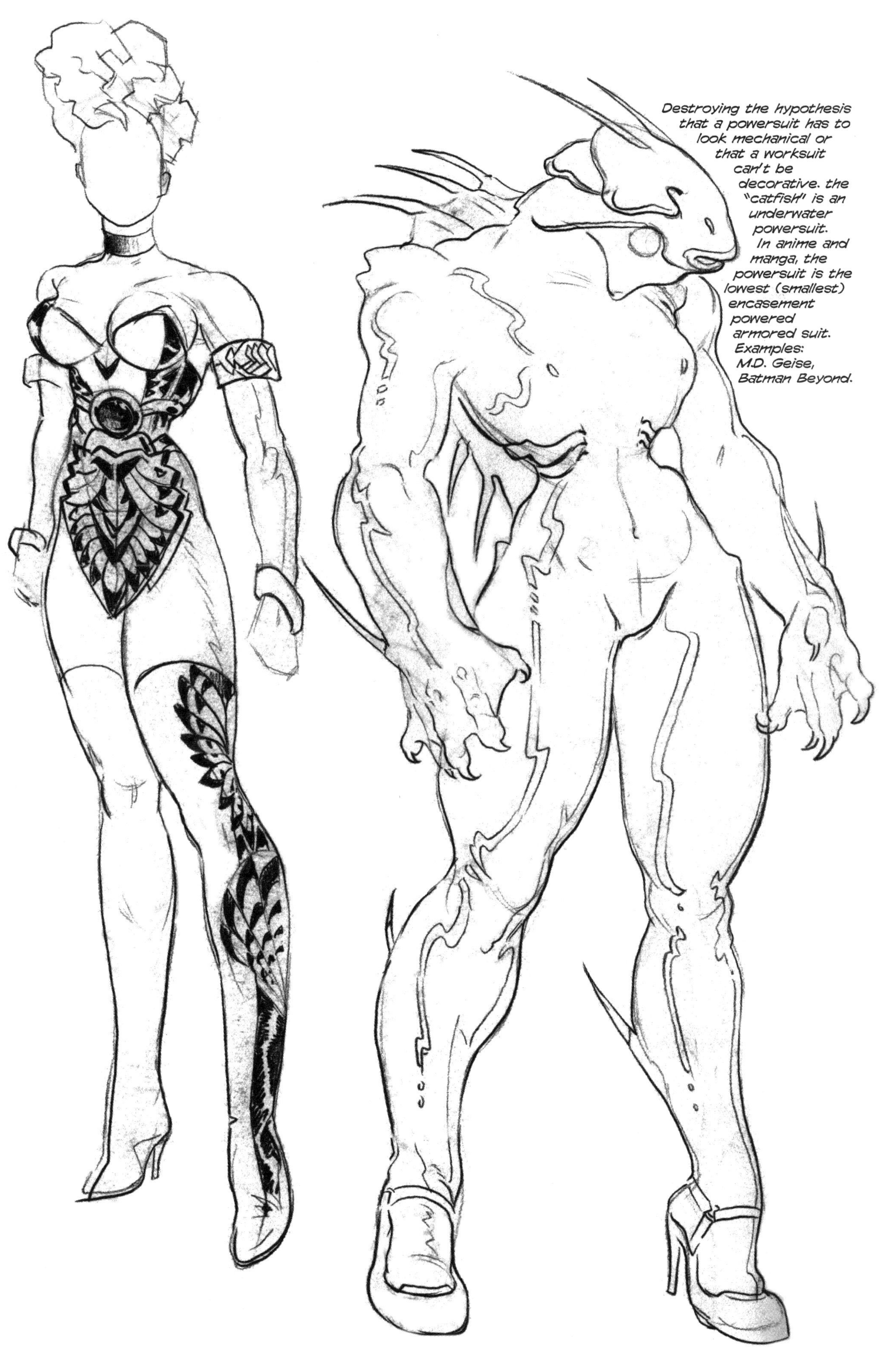

Destroying the hypothesis that a powersuit has to look mechanical or that a worksuit can't be decorative. the "catfish" is an underwater powersuit. In anime and manga, the powersuit is the lowest (smallest) encasement powered armored suit. Examples: M.D. Geise, Batman Beyond.

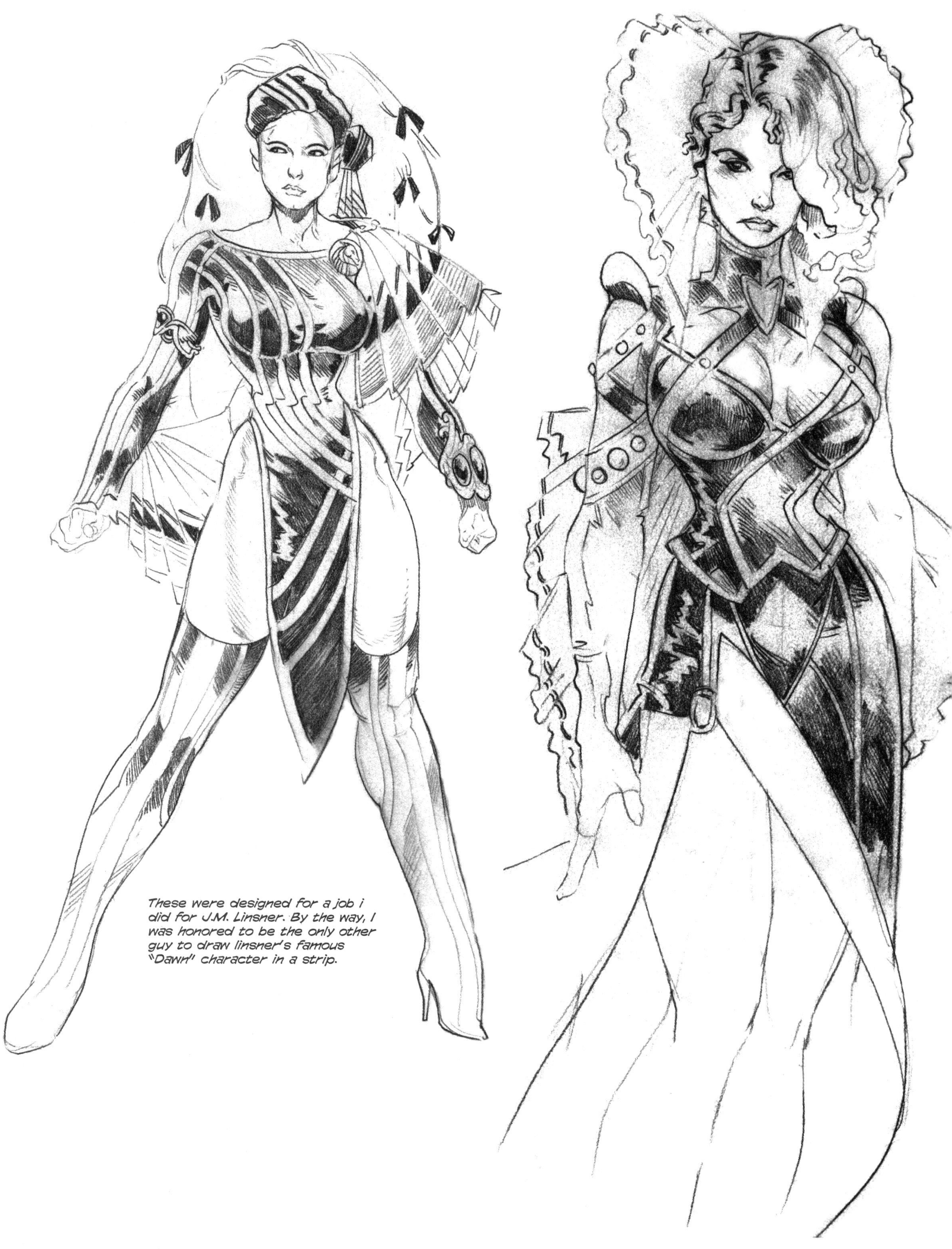

These were designed for a job i did for J.M. Linsner. By the way, I was honored to be the only other guy to draw linsner's famous "Dawn" character in a strip.

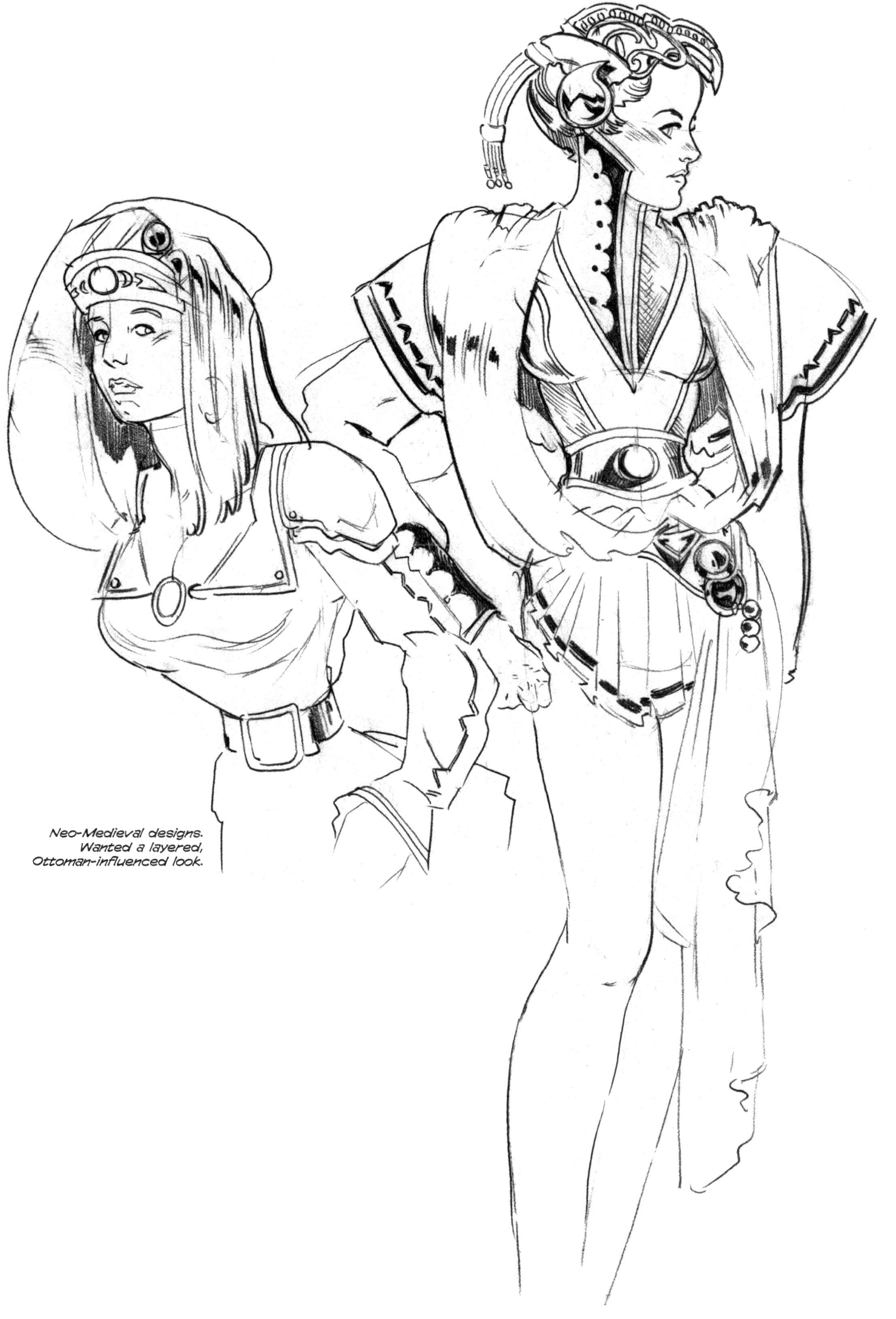

Neo-Medieval designs.
Wanted a layered,
Ottoman-influenced look.

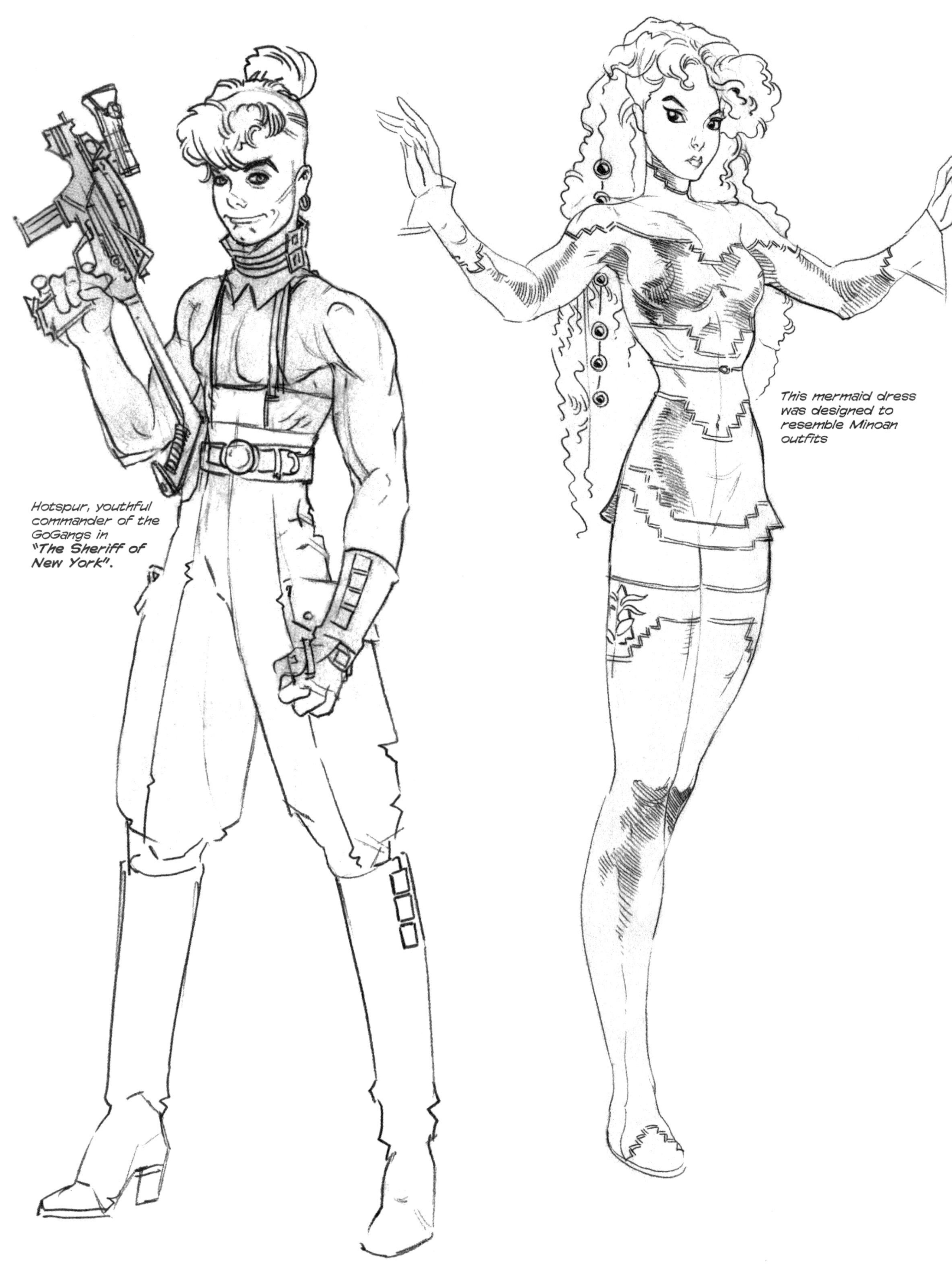
Hotspur, youthful commander of the GoGangs in **"The Sheriff of New York"**.
This mermaid dress was designed to resemble Minoan outfits

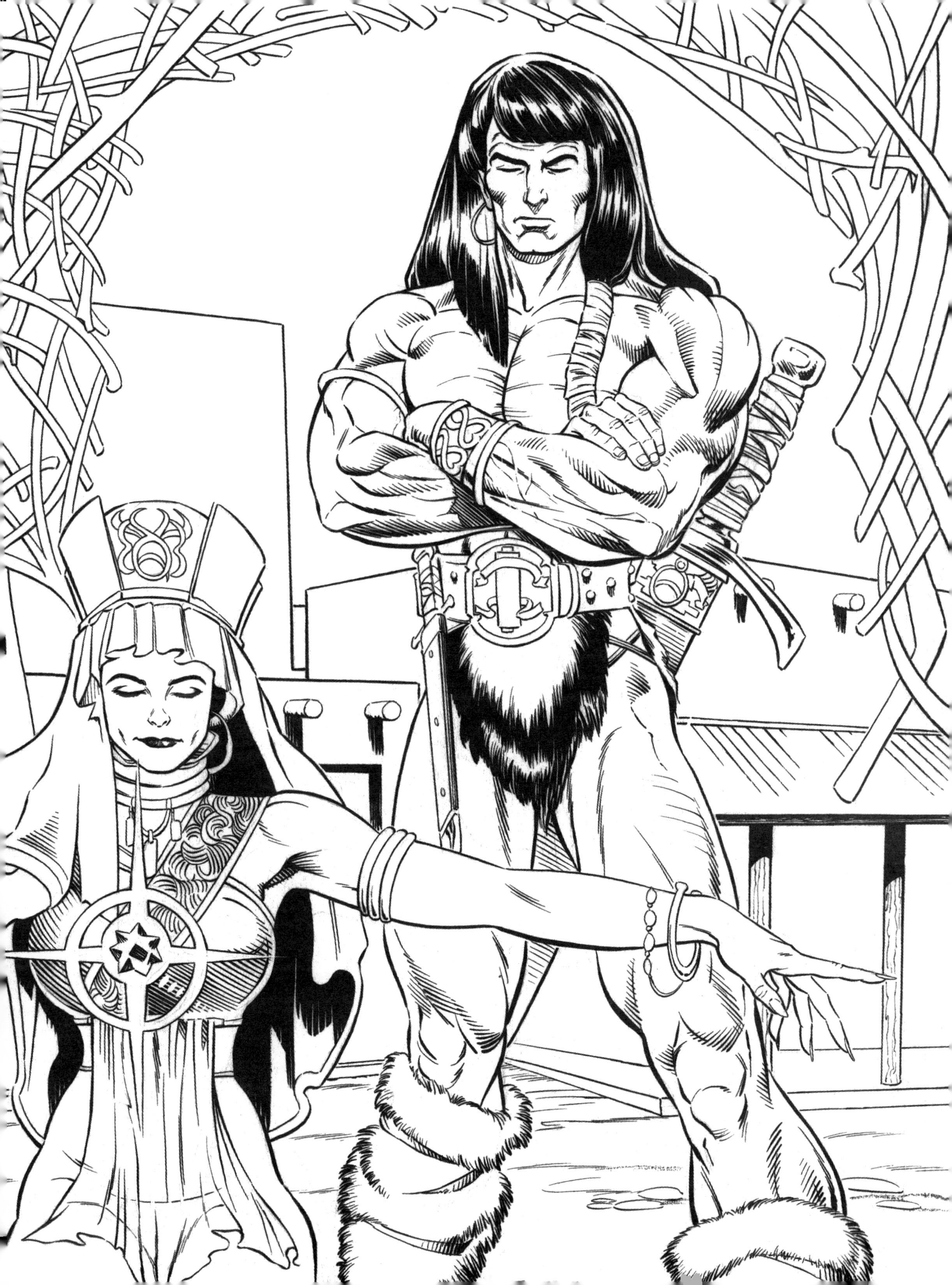

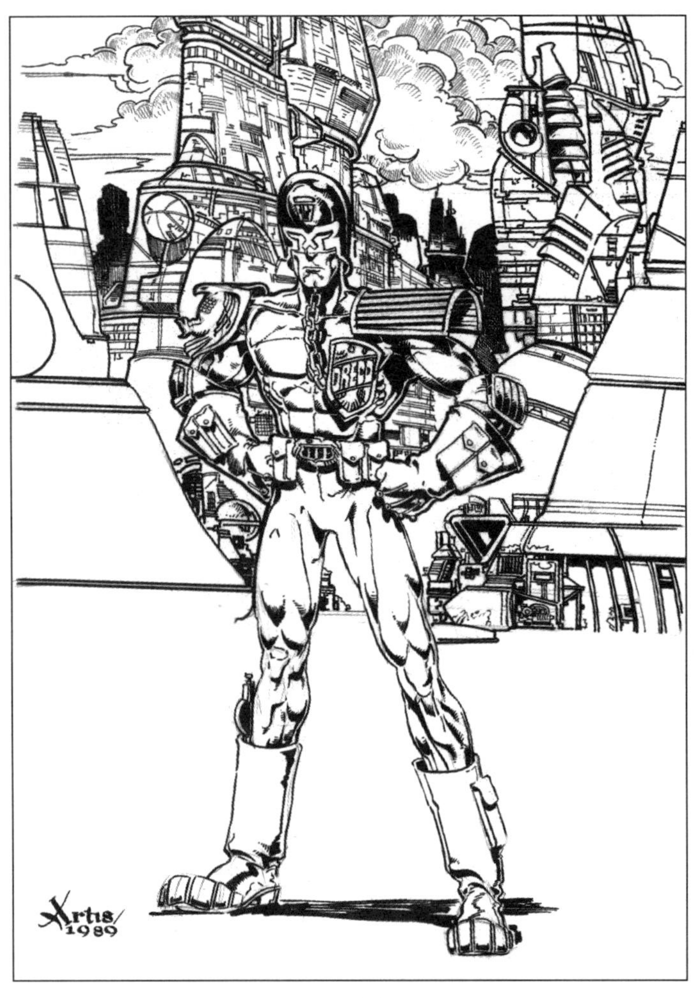

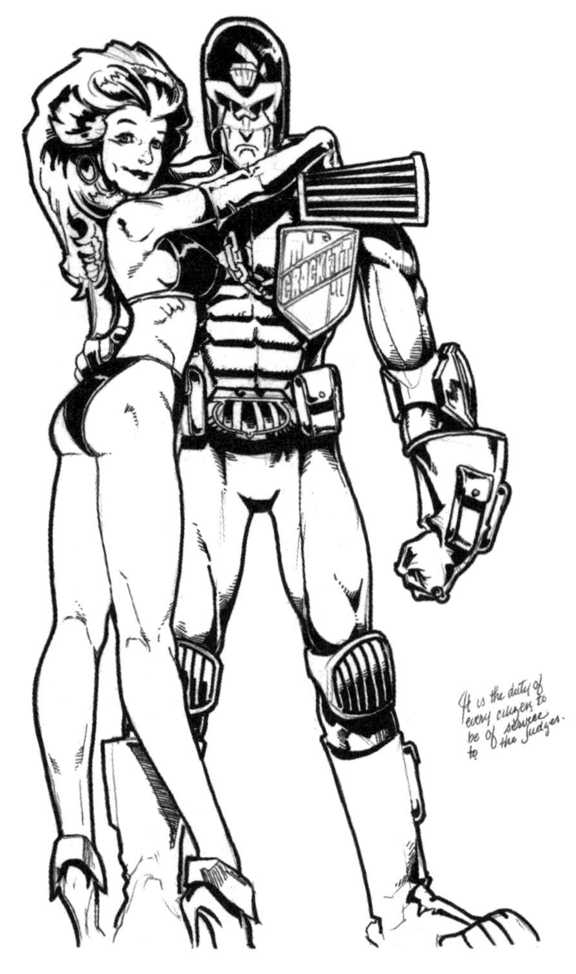

Dredd tests

Done while I worked for DC, this awkward looking Dredd followed the superhero style they encouraged me to work in.

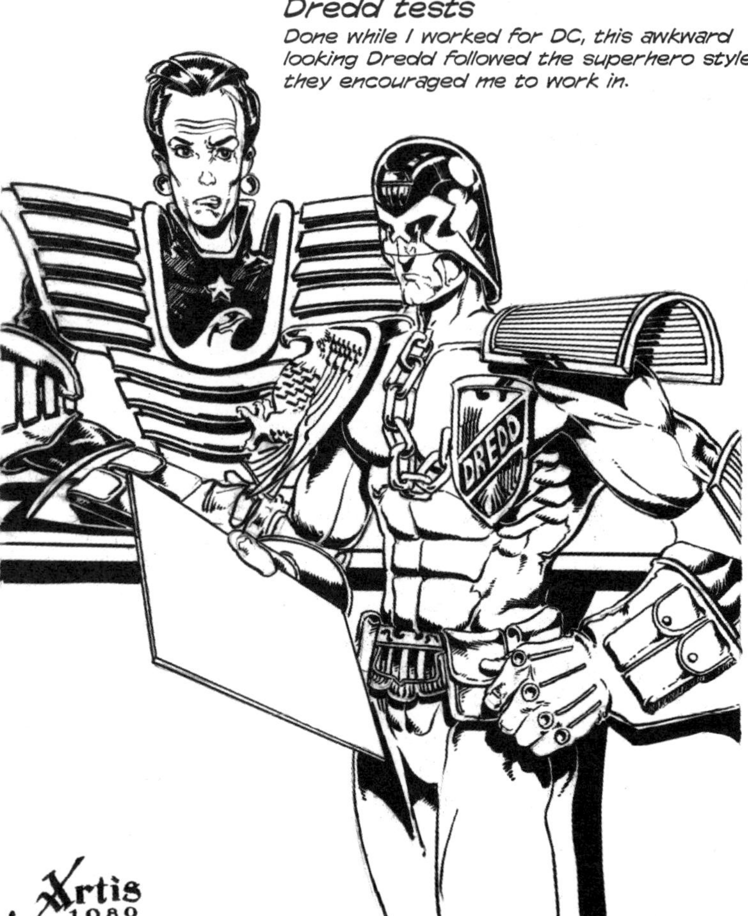

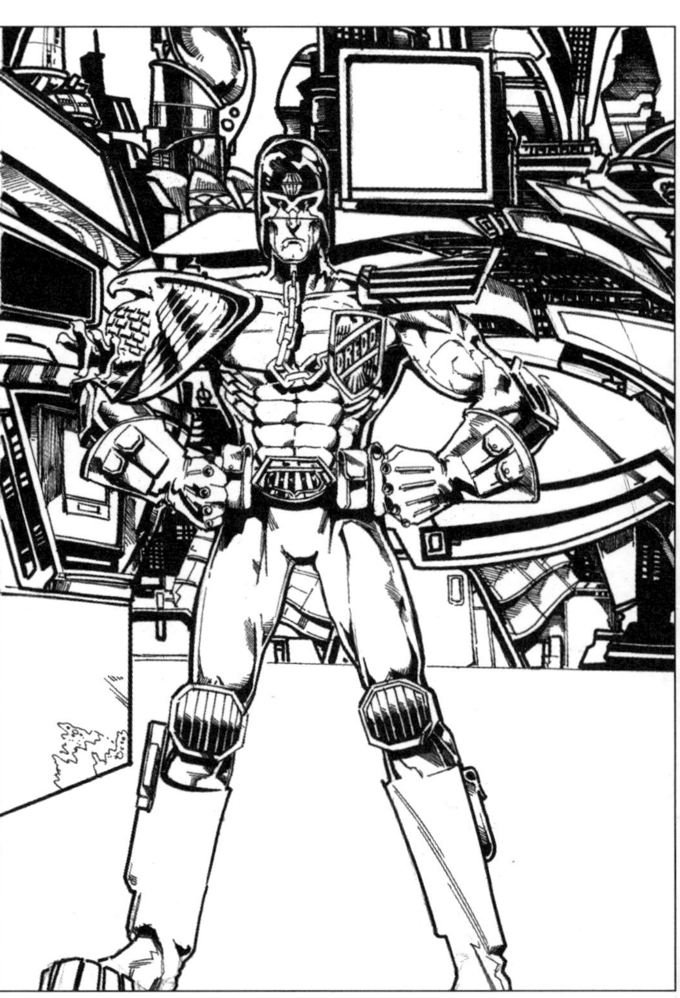

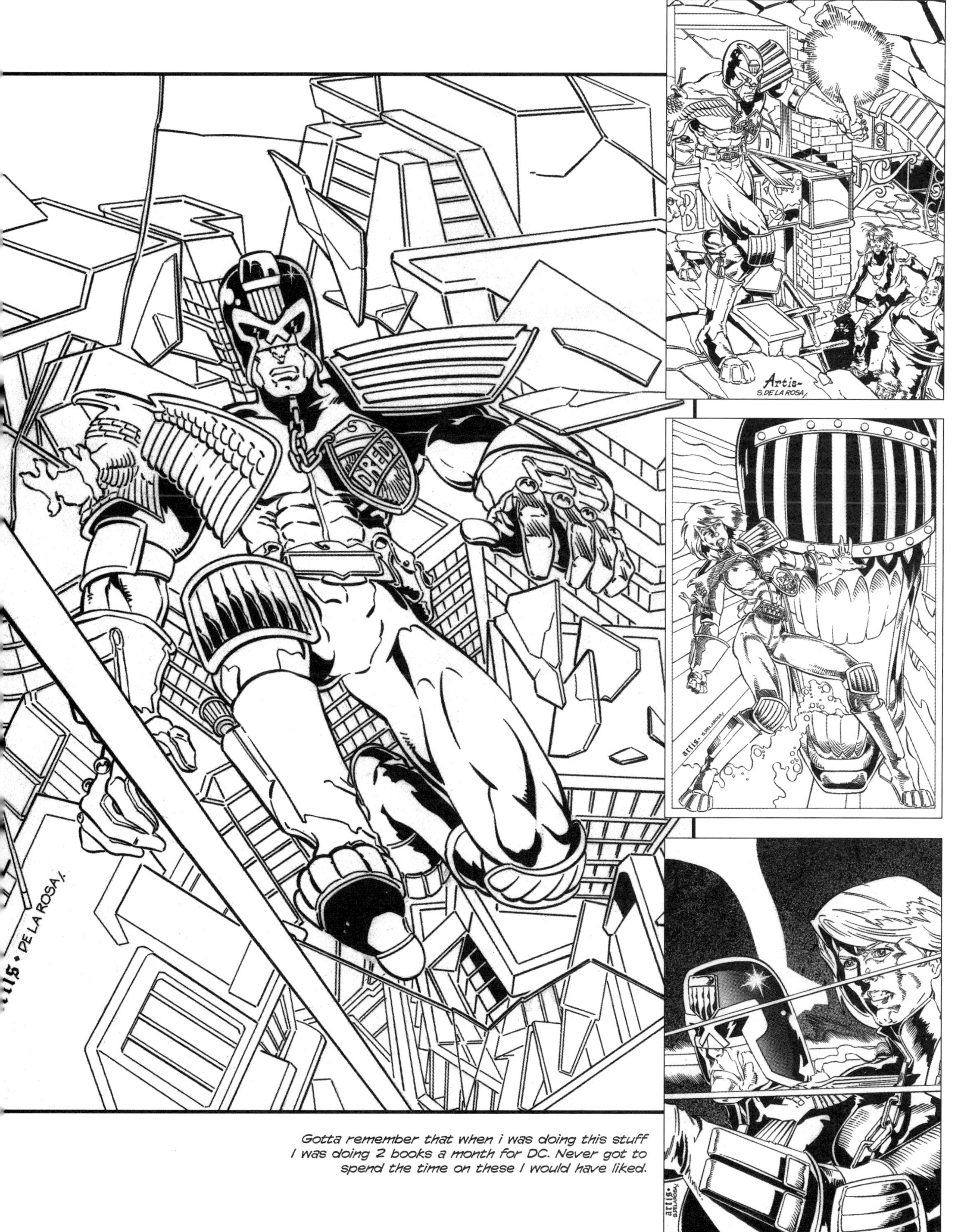

Gotta remember that when i was doing this stuff I was doing 2 books a month for DC. Never got to spend the time on these I would have liked.

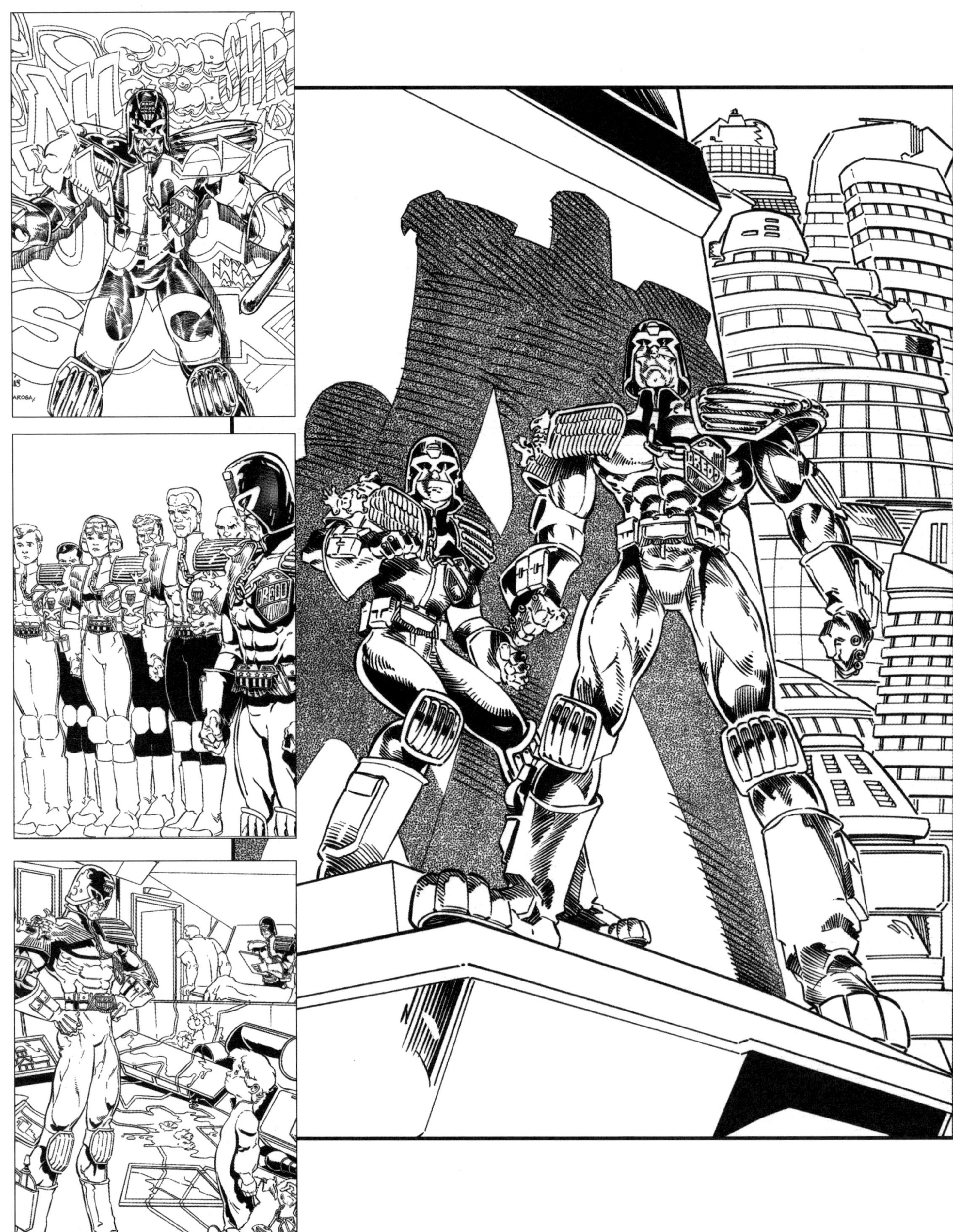
DREDD

Sam de la Rosa's gorgeous inks saved this turkey..
.check out these "Ger ugly" sump fans.

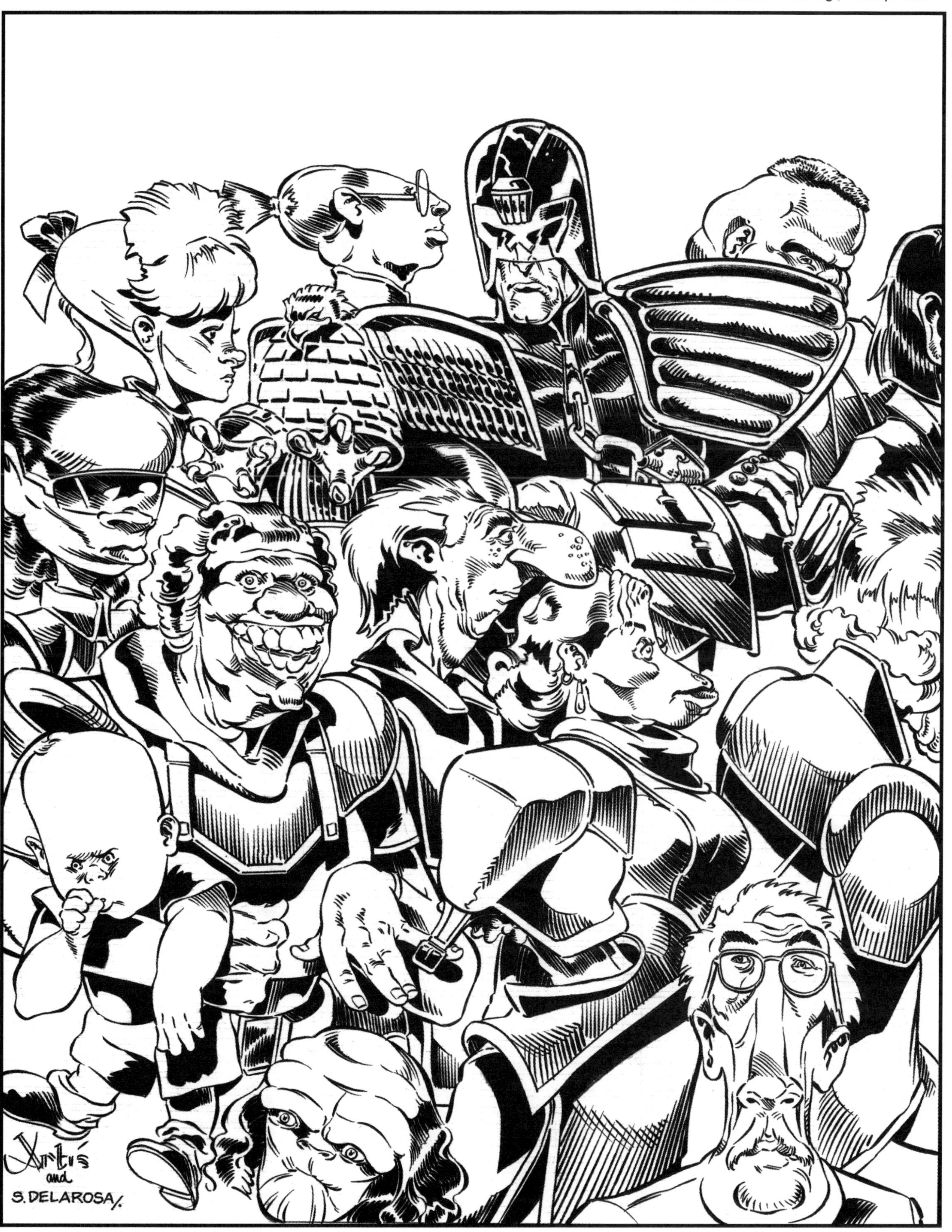

This cover, probably the best I did for Quality Comics, worked because of the compositional strength of the bad guy suit.

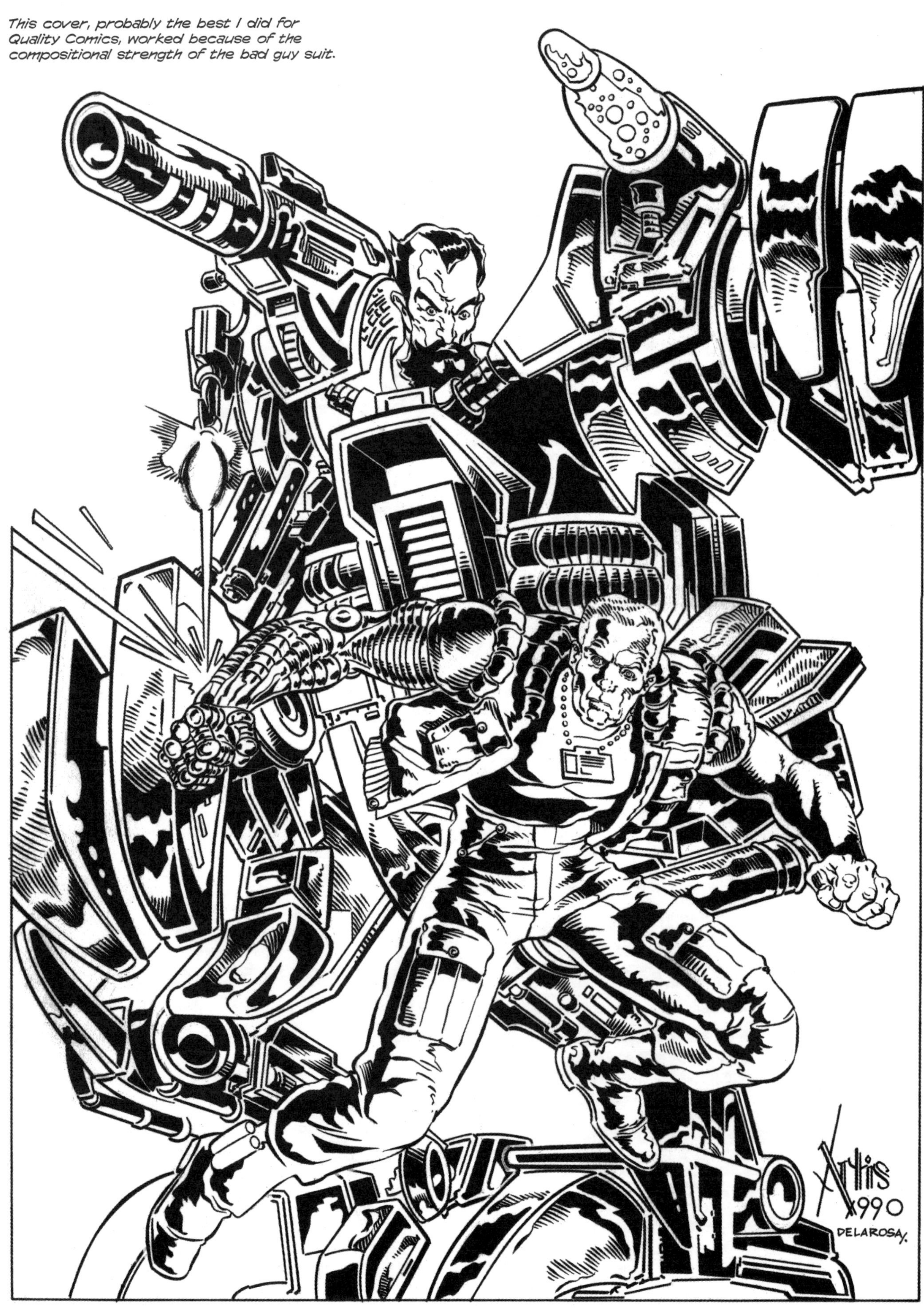

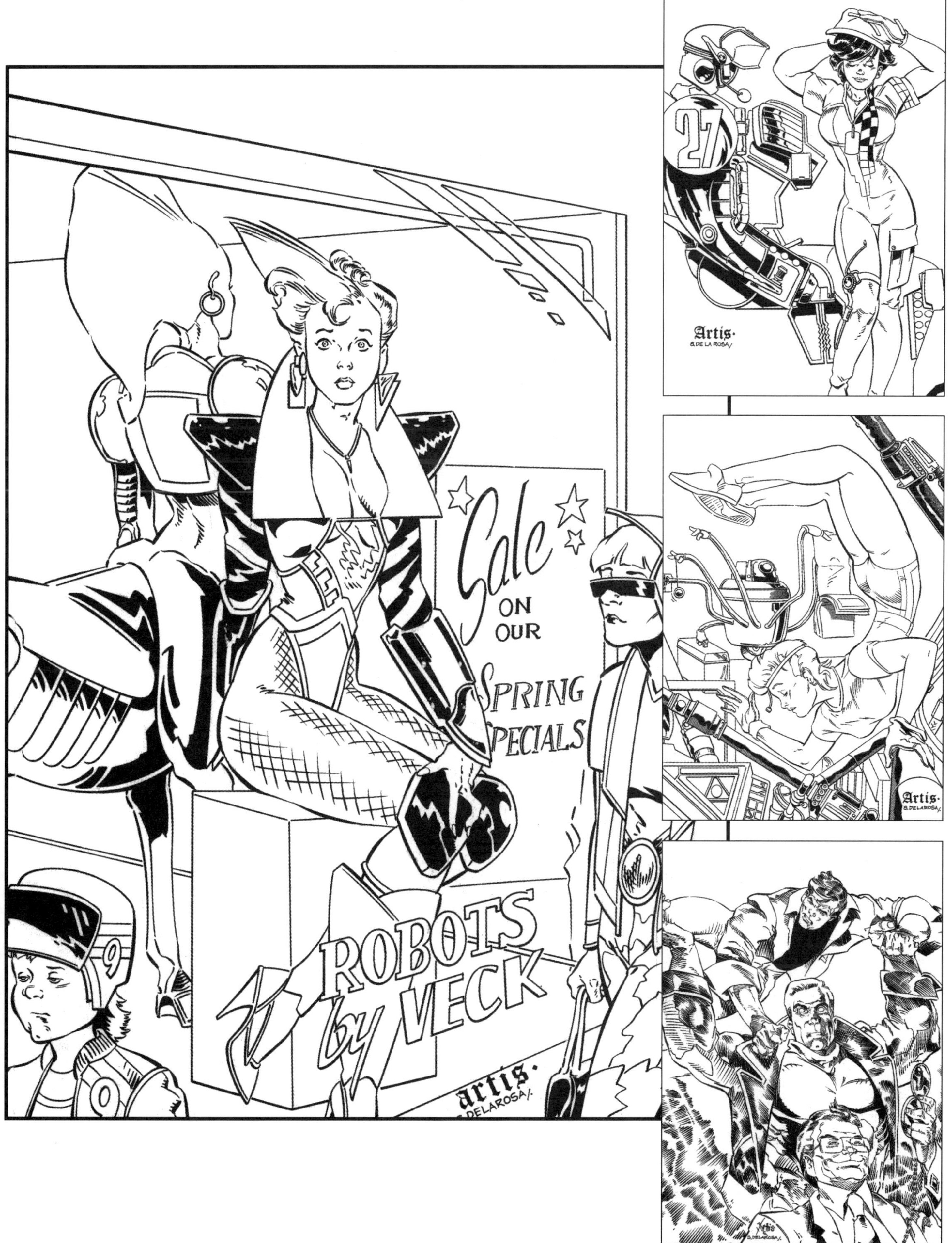
Sale
ON
OUR
SPRING
SPECIALS
ROBOTS
by VECK
artis.
S.DELAROSA/.
27
Artis.
S. DE LA ROSA/
Artis.
S.DELAROSA/.

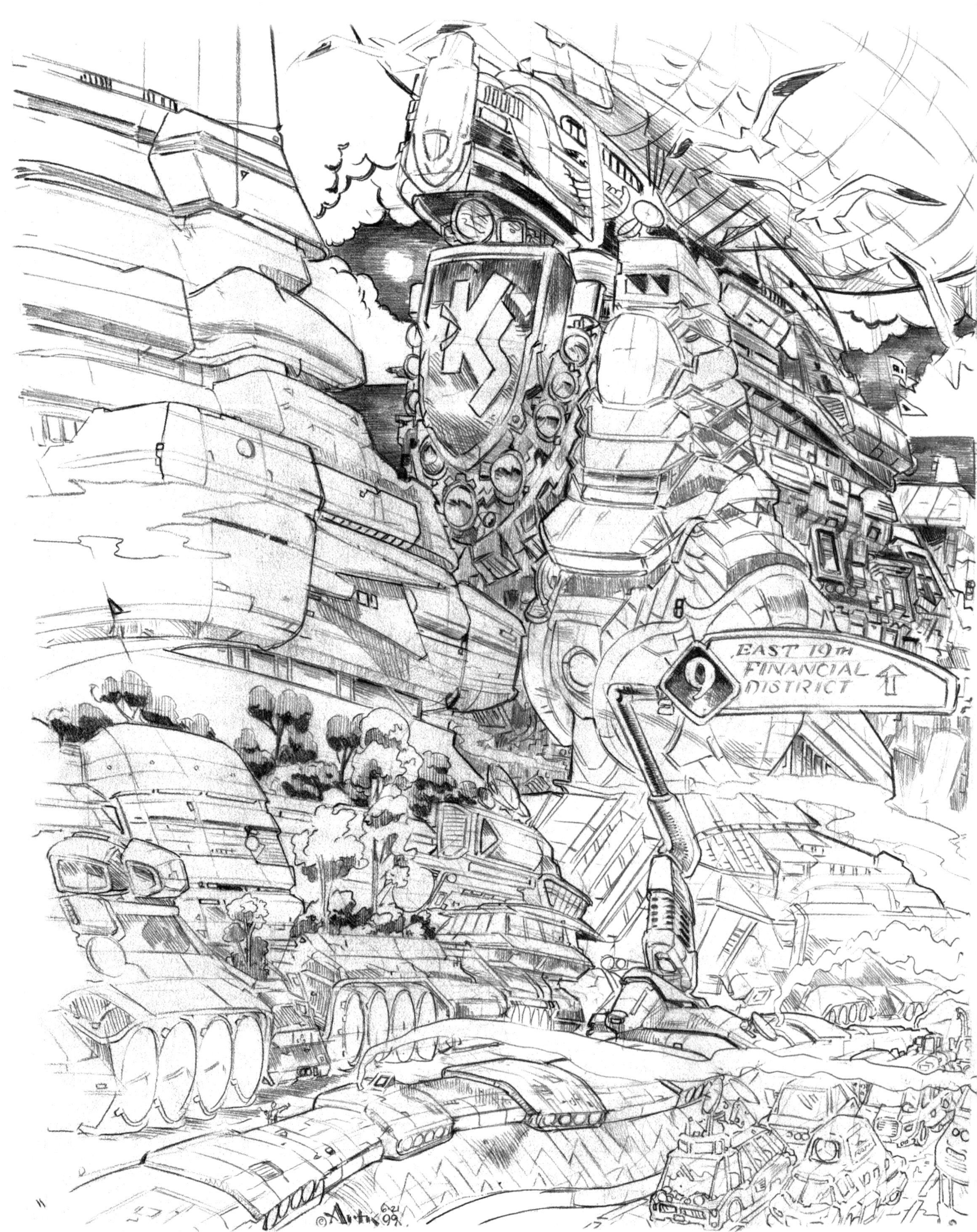

Detroit One

In Detroit 2200+, the last "Free City" in the future USA, the buildings are motorized and move every day. Without a daily roadmap, you can't fight city hall, because it moves every day.

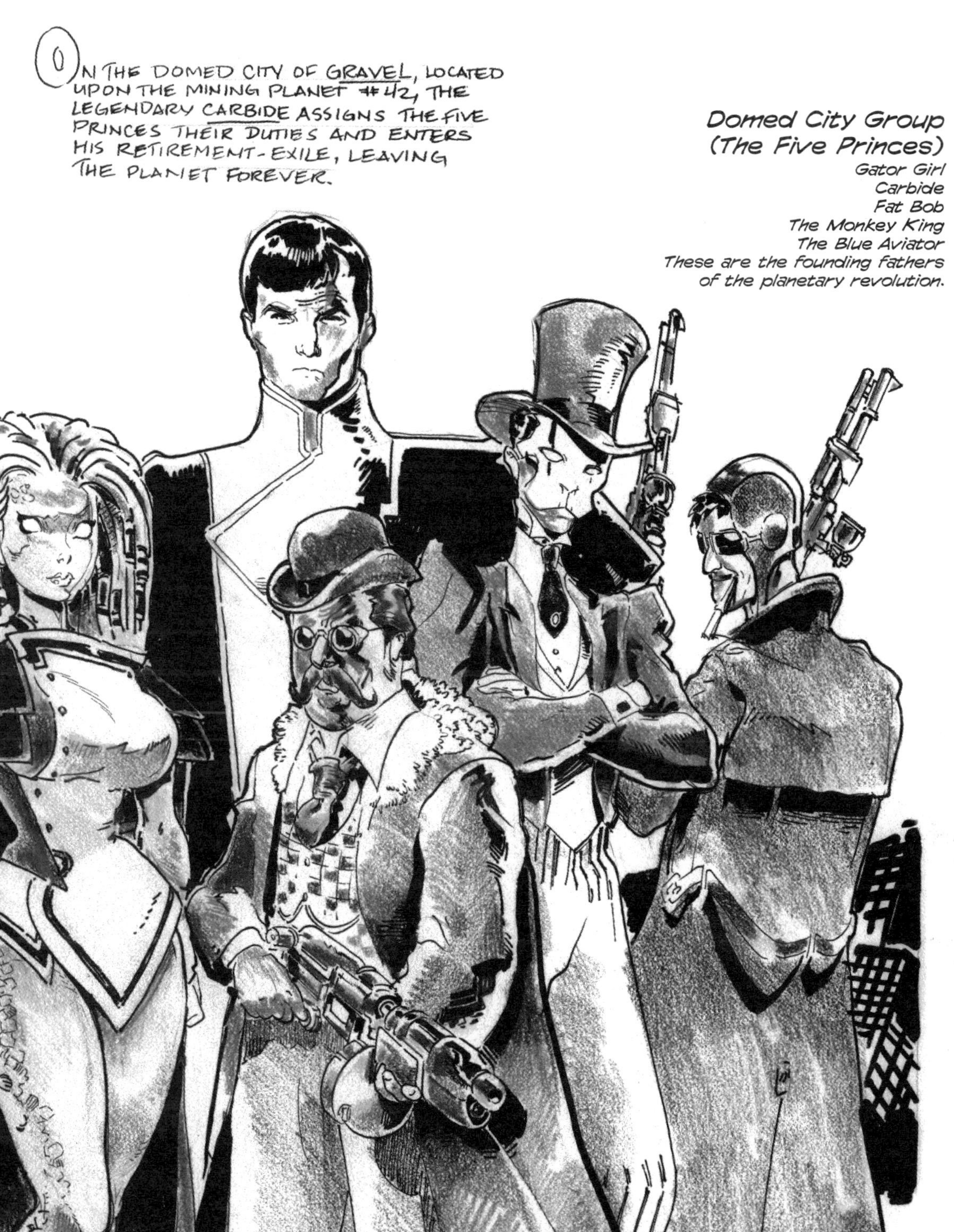

Domed City Group
(The Five Princes)
Gator Girl
Carbide
Fat Bob
The Monkey King
The Blue Aviator
These are the founding fathers of the planetary revolution.

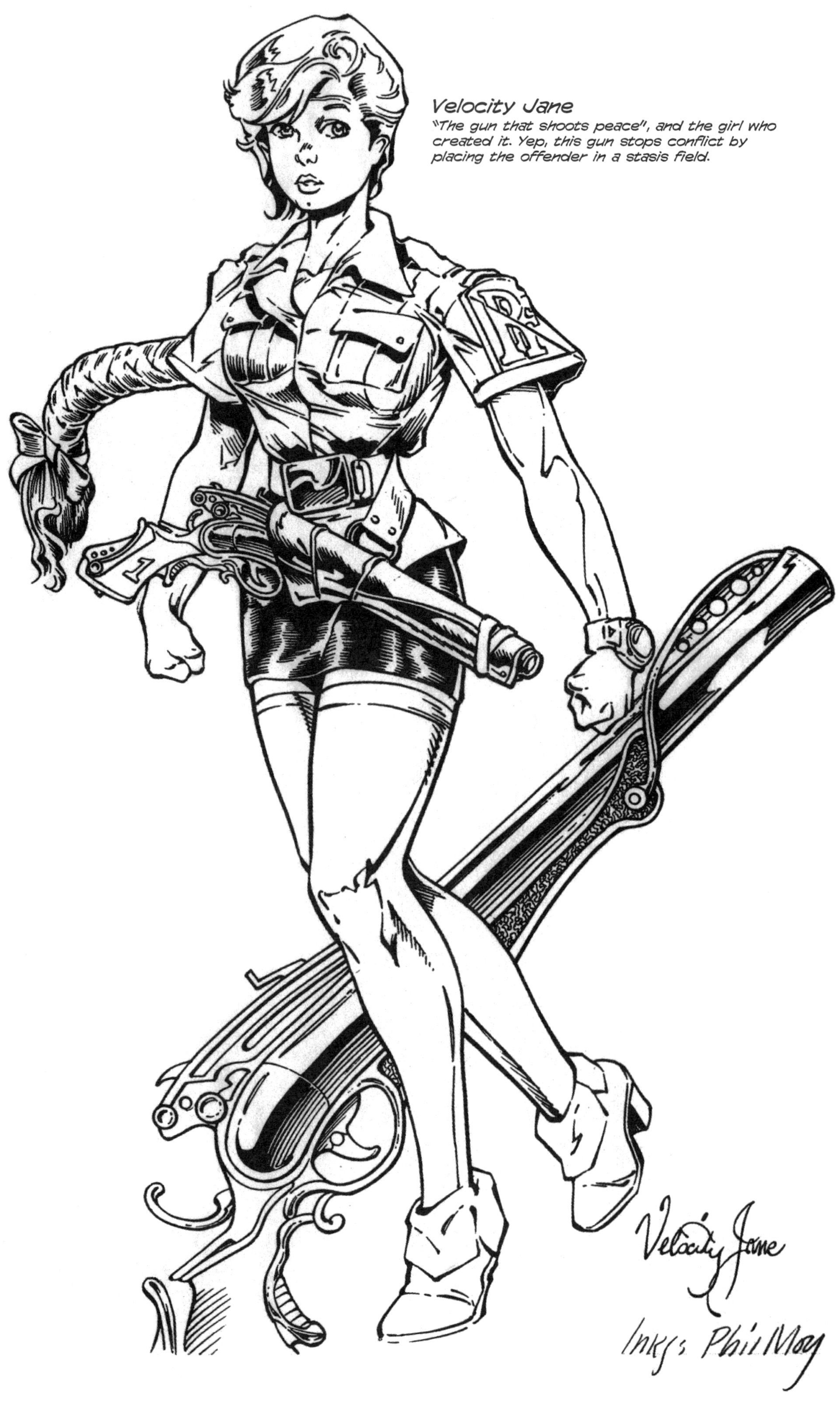

Velocity Jane

"The gun that shoots peace", and the girl who created it. Yep, this gun stops conflict by placing the offender in a stasis field.

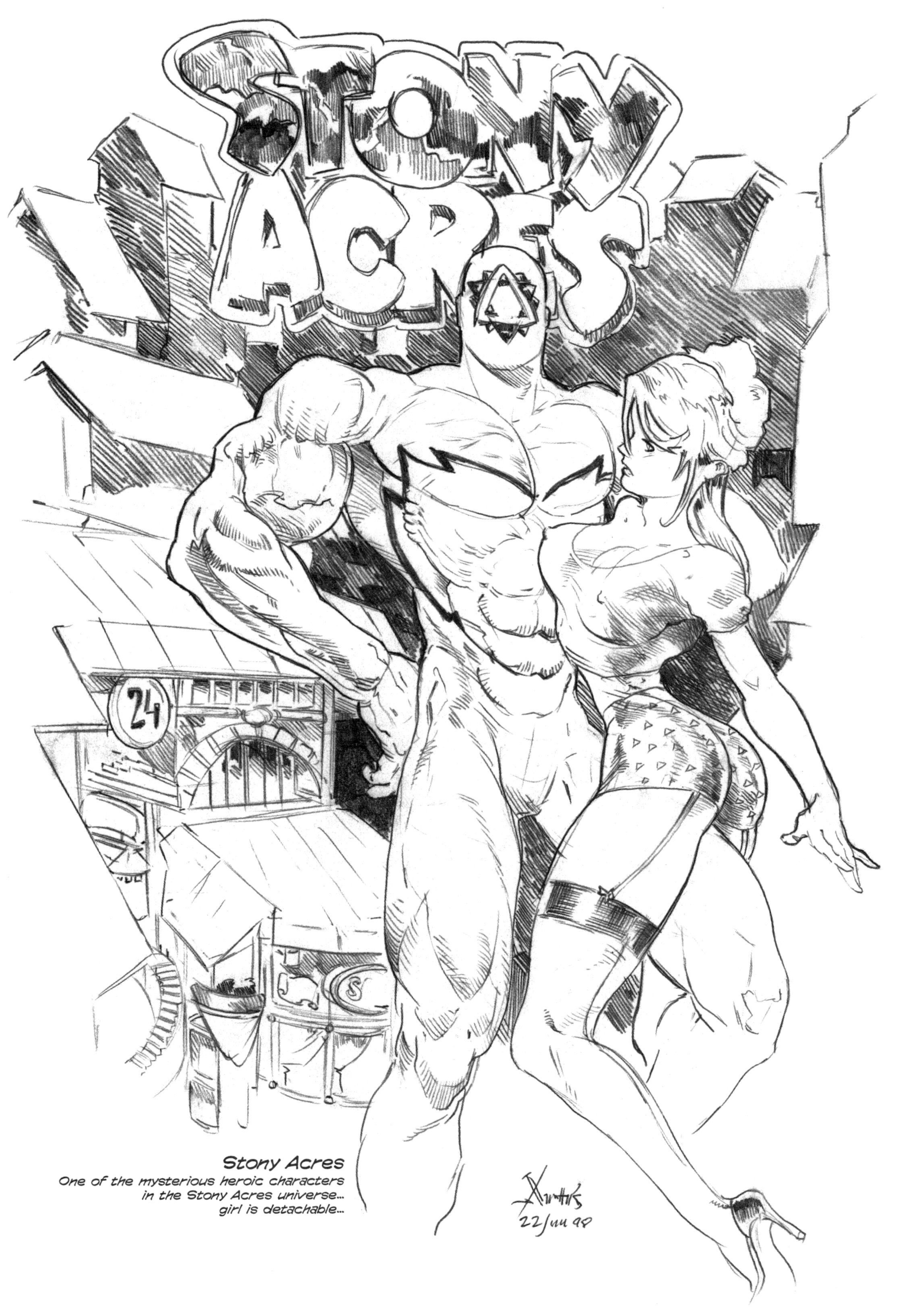

Stony Acres

One of the mysterious heroic characters in the Stony Acres universe... girl is detachable...

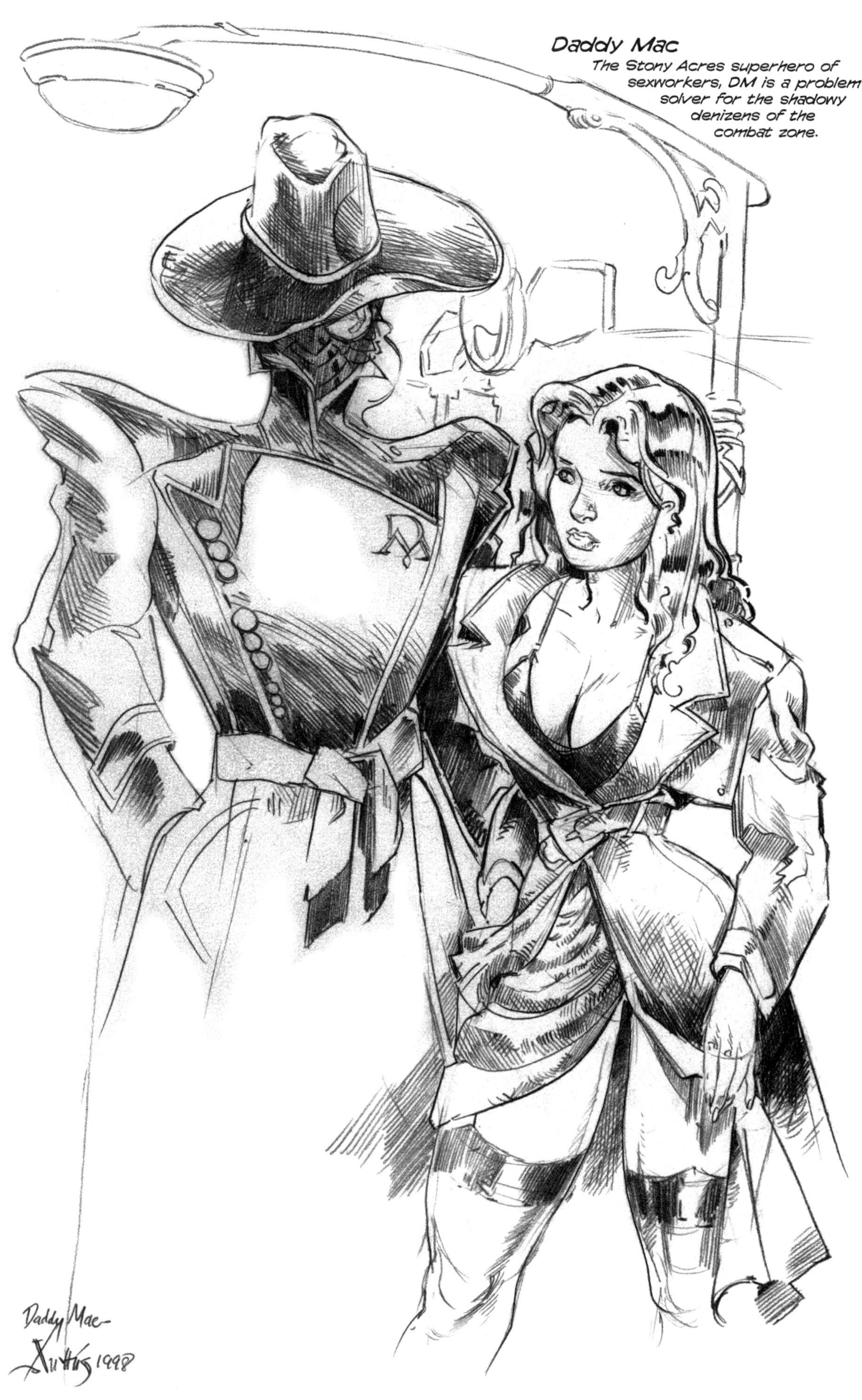
Daddy Mac
The Stony Acres superhero of sexworkers, DM is a problem solver for the shadowy denizens of the combat zone.
DM
Daddy Mac
1998

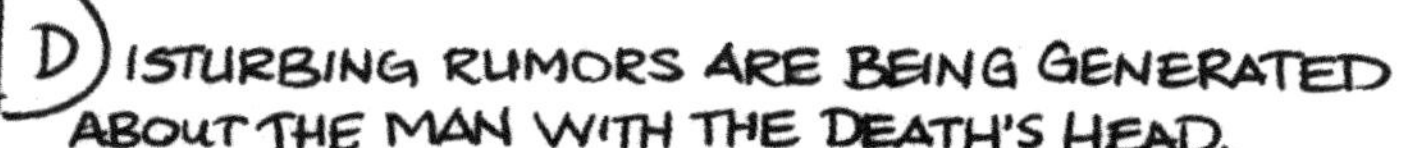

DISTURBING RUMORS ARE BEING GENERATED ABOUT THE MAN WITH THE DEATH'S HEAD.

NOT ONLY ARE FRIGHTENING AND TRULY BIZARRE MONSTERS COMING FROM HIS TERROR-LABS IN STONY ACRES, BUT THERE IS A WHISPER ON THE STREET THAT BONES HAS CREATED A WHOLE NEW STYLE OF SYNTHETIC LIFE.

SECURE IN HIS STRONGHOLD, FEARED BY THE INHABITANTS, MISTER BONES IS IN CHARGE.

CAN EVEN SUMMONING THE FIVE PRINCES STOP HIM? WE'LL SEE...

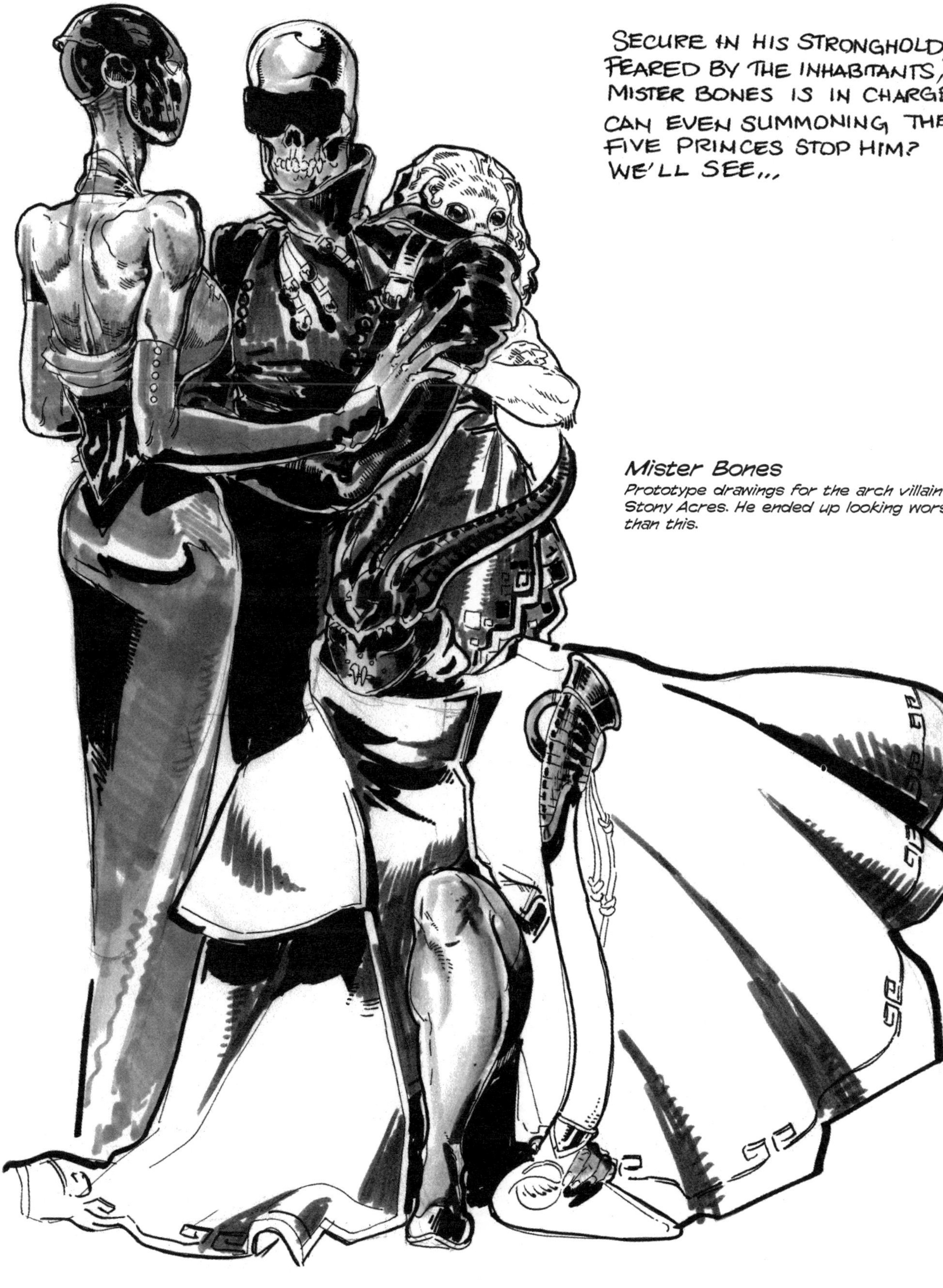

Mister Bones

Prototype drawings for the arch villain of Stony Acres. He ended up looking worse than this.

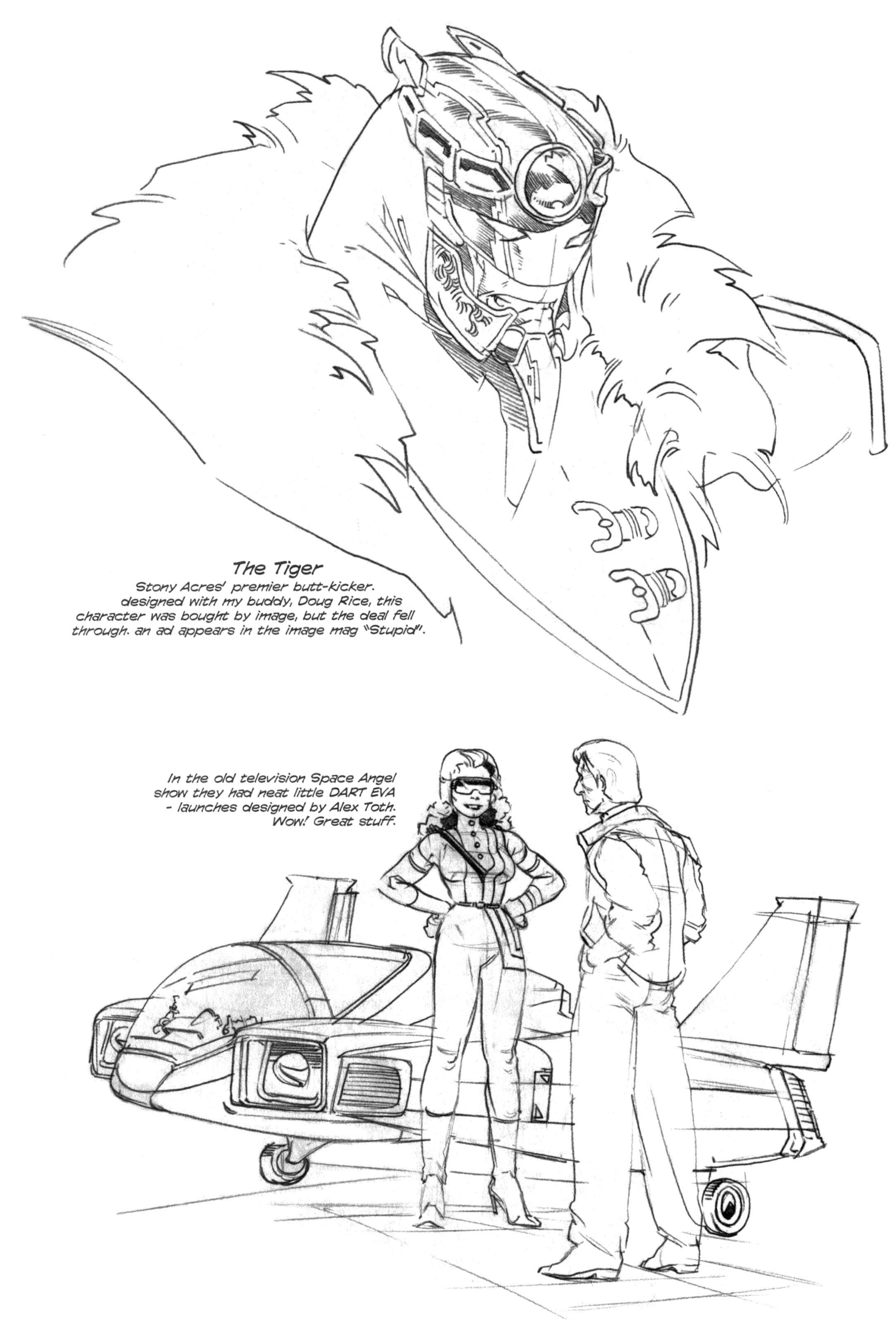

The Tiger
Stony Acres' premier butt-kicker. designed with my buddy, Doug Rice, this character was bought by image, but the deal fell through. an ad appears in the image mag "Stupid".

In the old television Space Angel show they had neat little DART EVA - launches designed by Alex Toth. Wow! Great stuff.

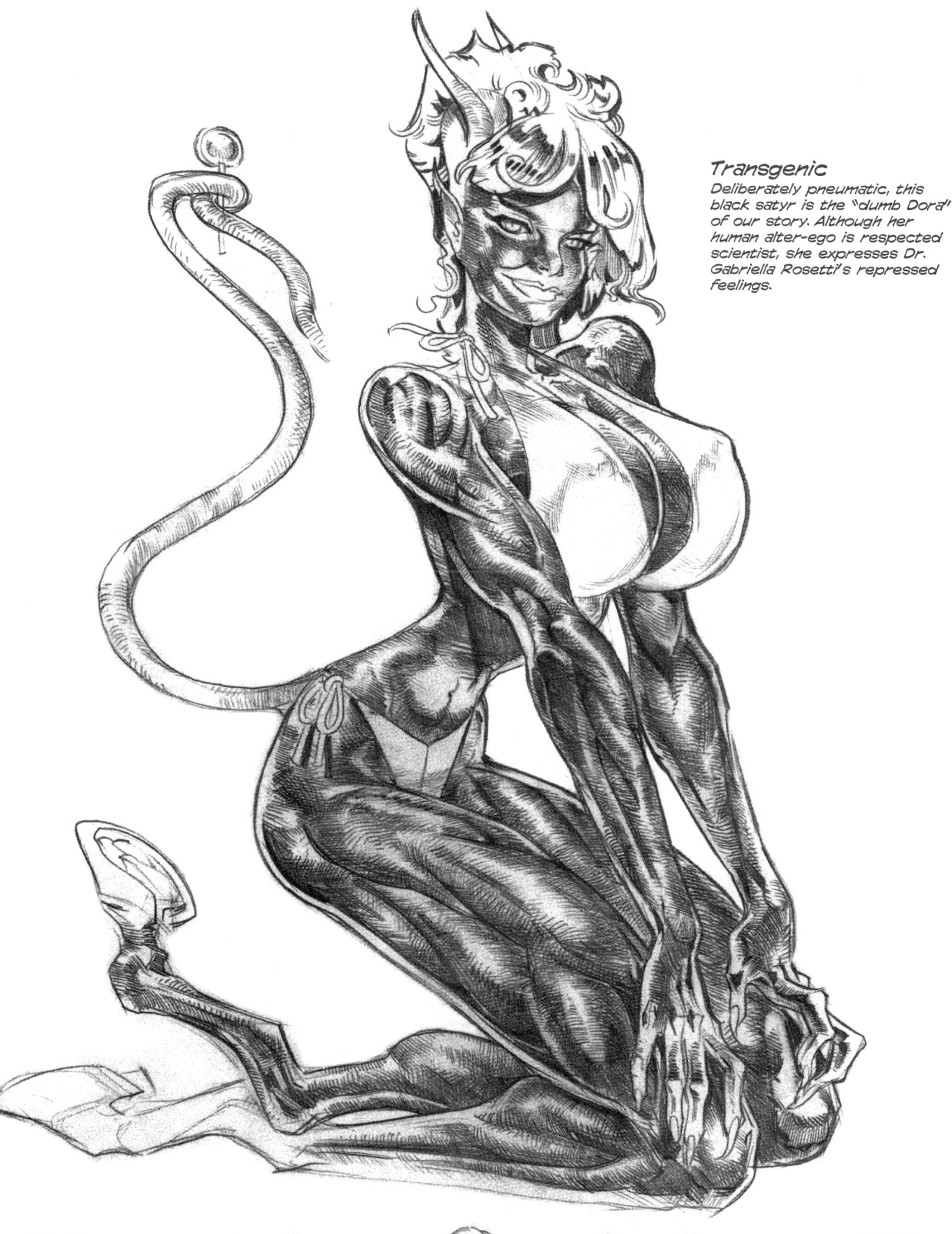

Transgenic

Deliberately pneumatic, this black satyr is the "dumb Dora" of our story. Although her human alter-ego is respected scientist, she expresses Dr. Gabriella Rosetti's repressed feelings.

Although Dr. Gabriella Rosetti occasionally changes into this form, the real story is the doc's discovery of a DNA cluster which allows metamorphosis and the last colony of giants who send two dupes to protect the secret...

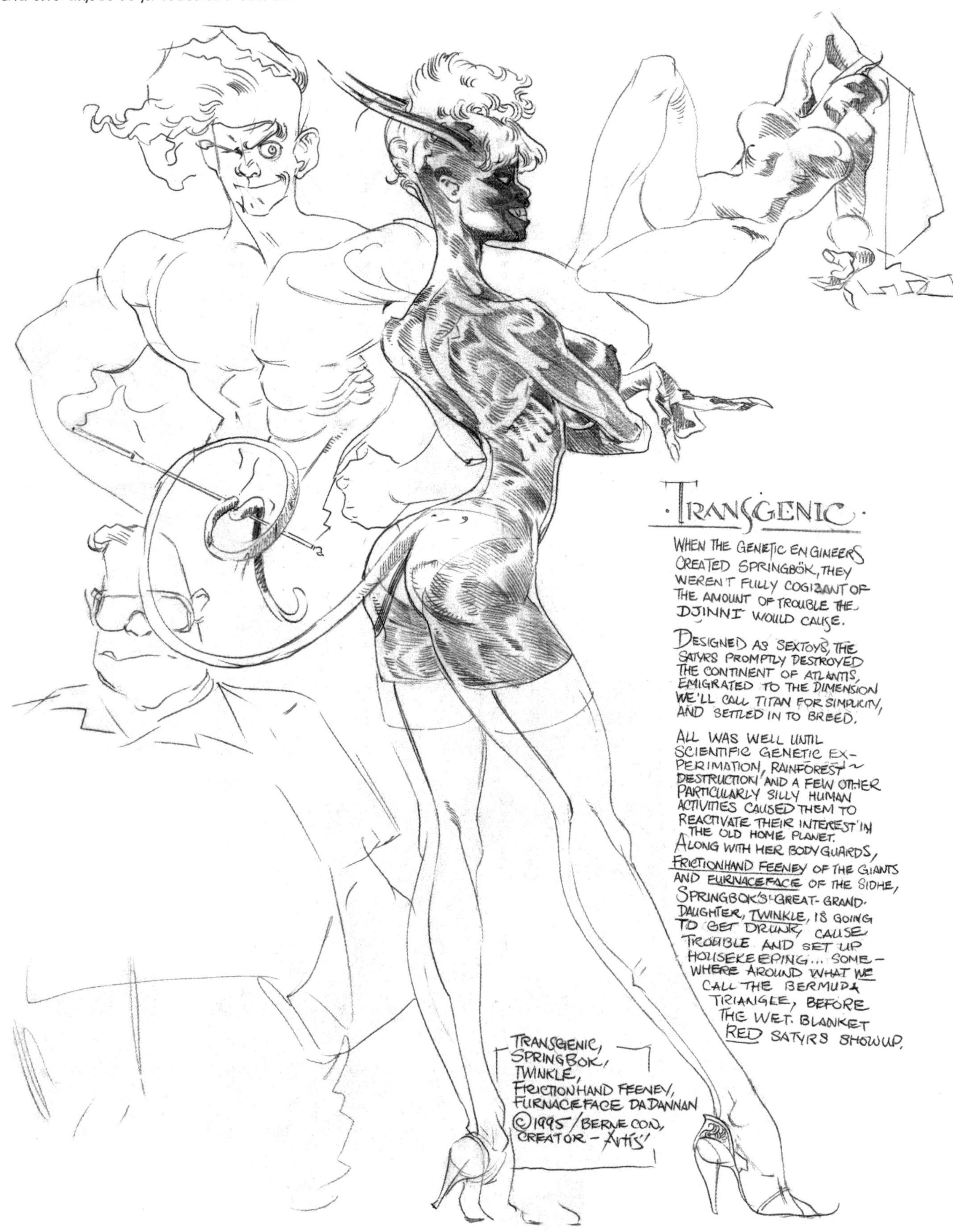

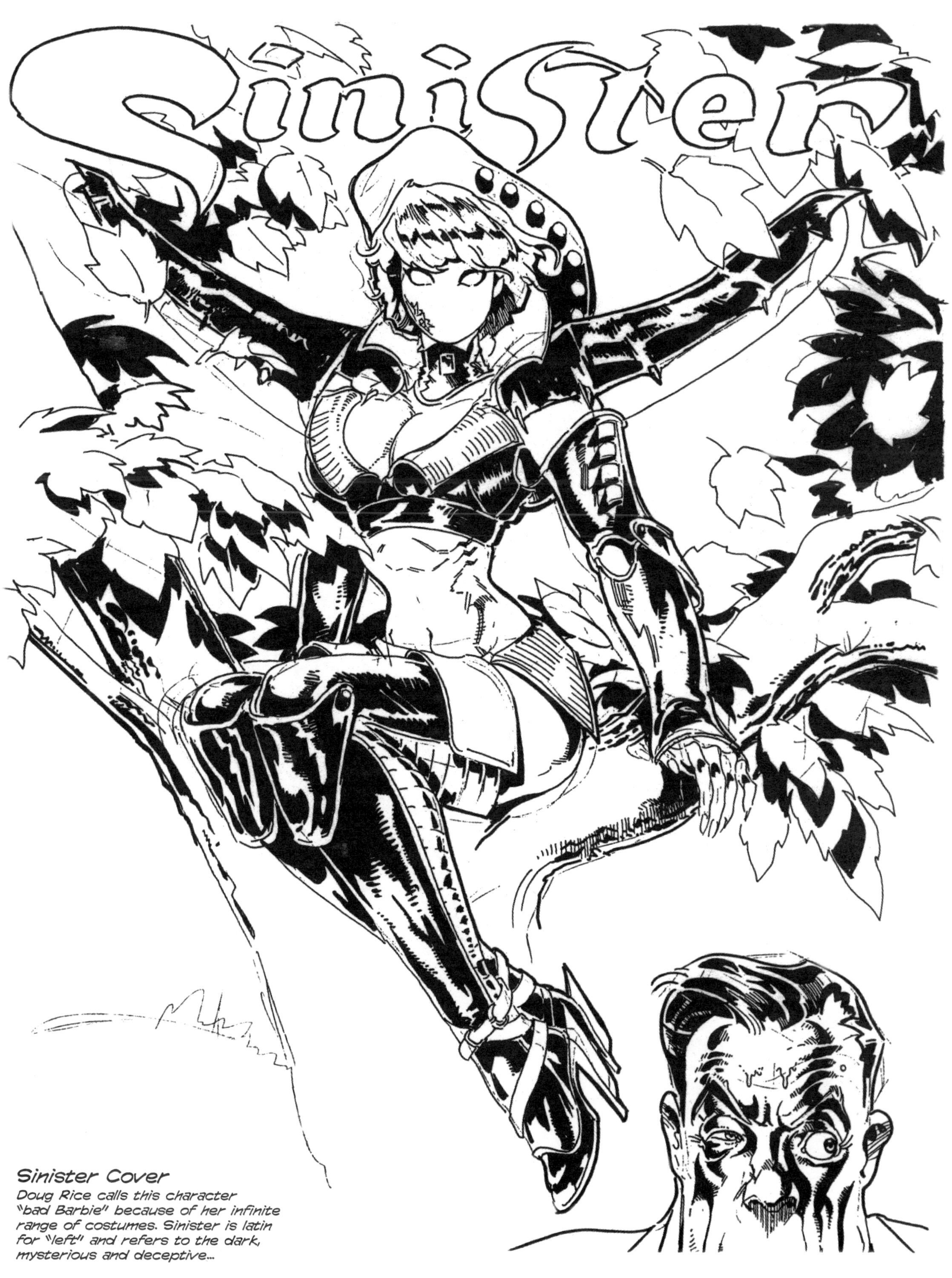

Sinister Cover

Doug Rice calls this character "bad Barbie" because of her infinite range of costumes. Sinister is latin for "left" and refers to the dark, mysterious and deceptive...

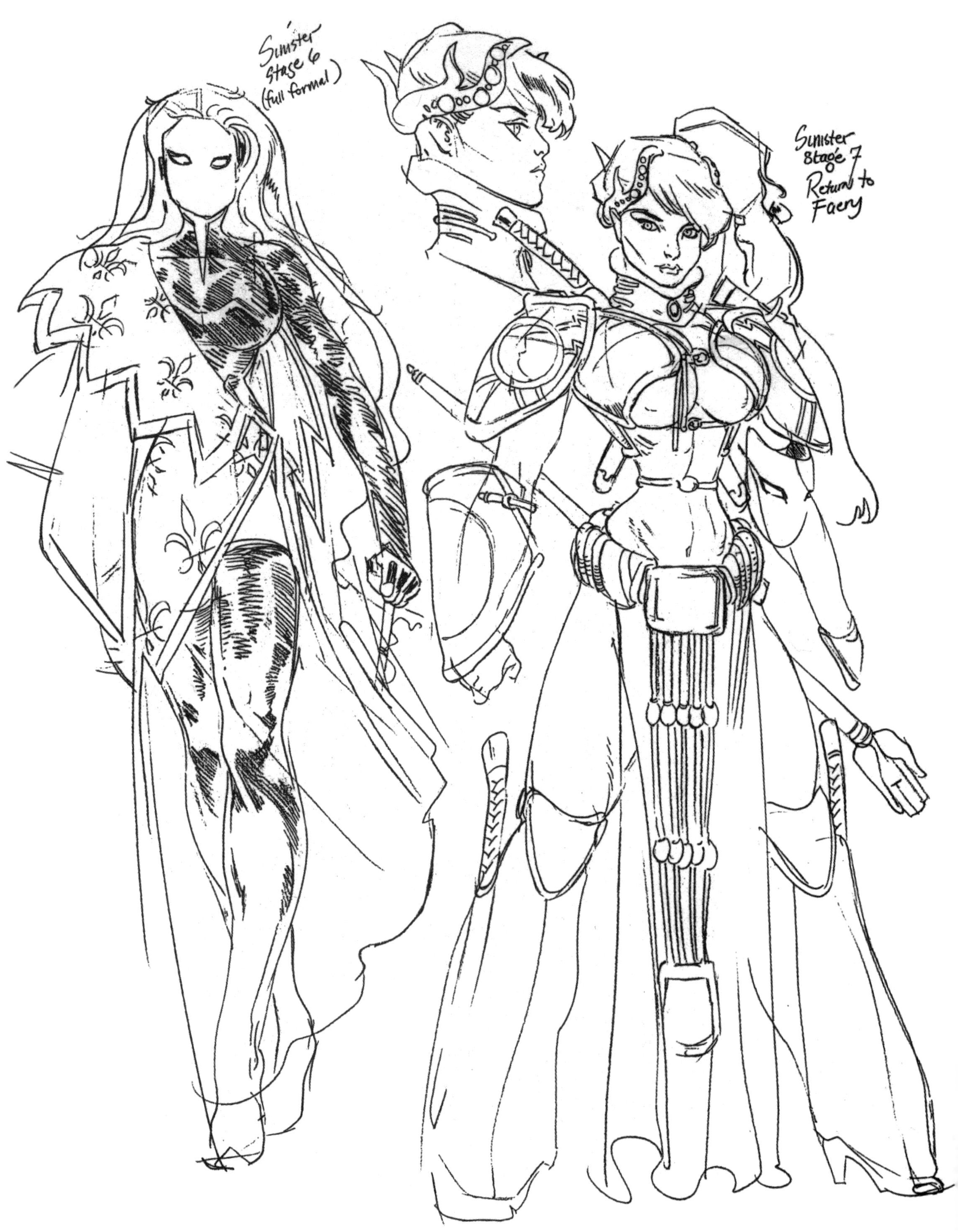
Sinister stage 6 (full formal)
Sinister stage 7 Return to Faery

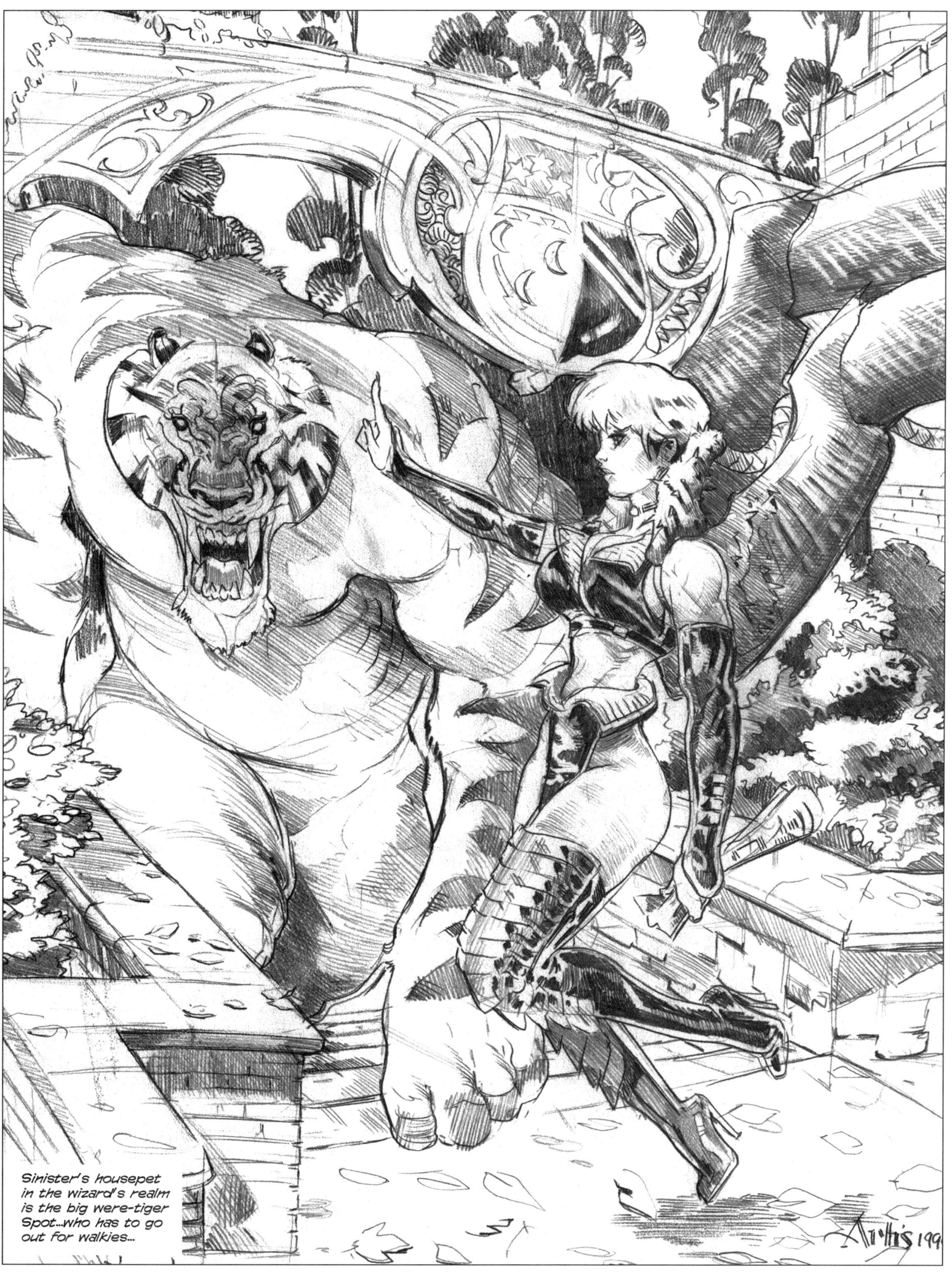
Sinister's housepet
in the wizard's realm
is the big were-tiger
Spot...who has to go
out for walkies...

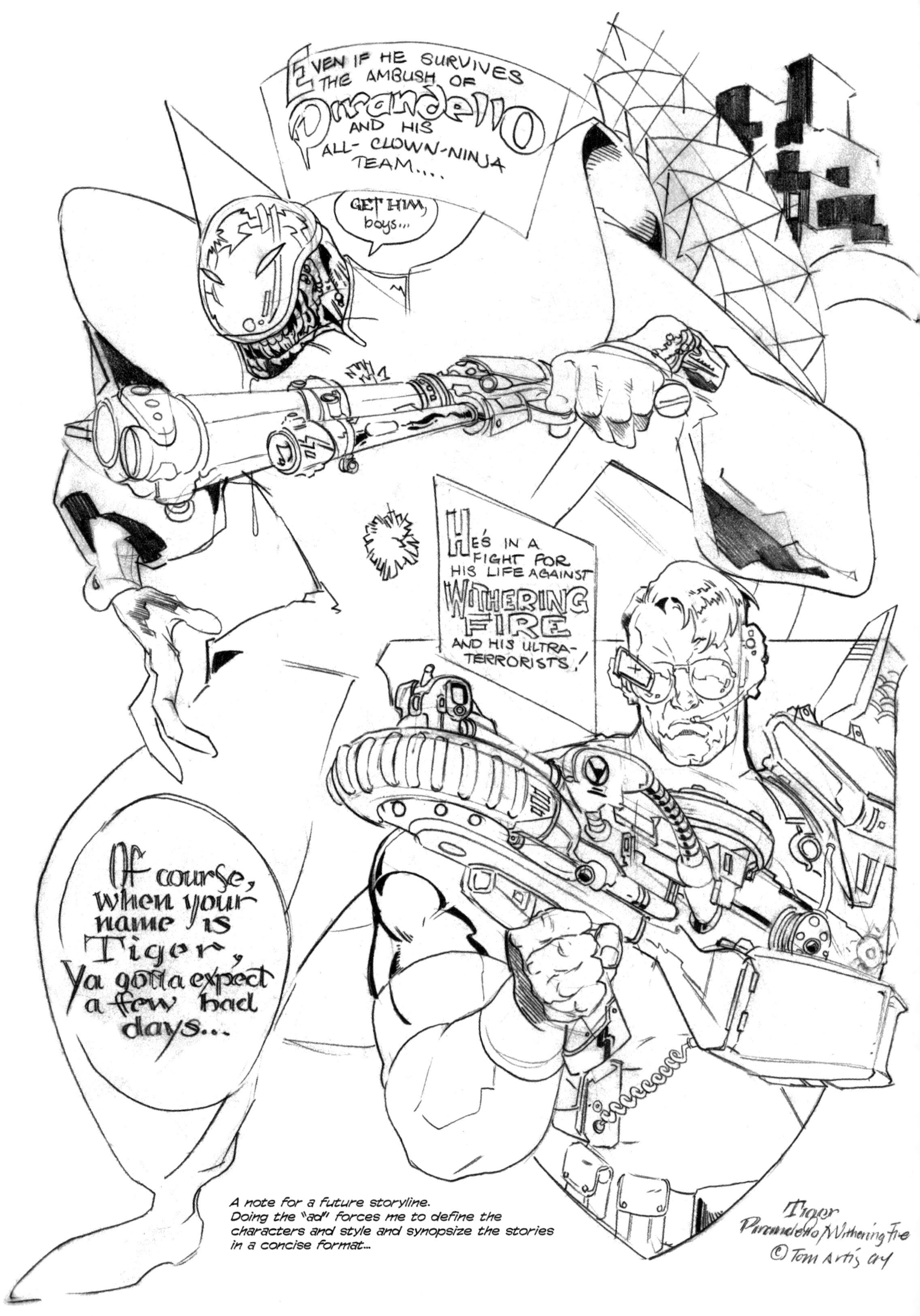

A note for a future storyline.
Doing the "ad" forces me to define the characters and style and synopsize the stories in a concise format...

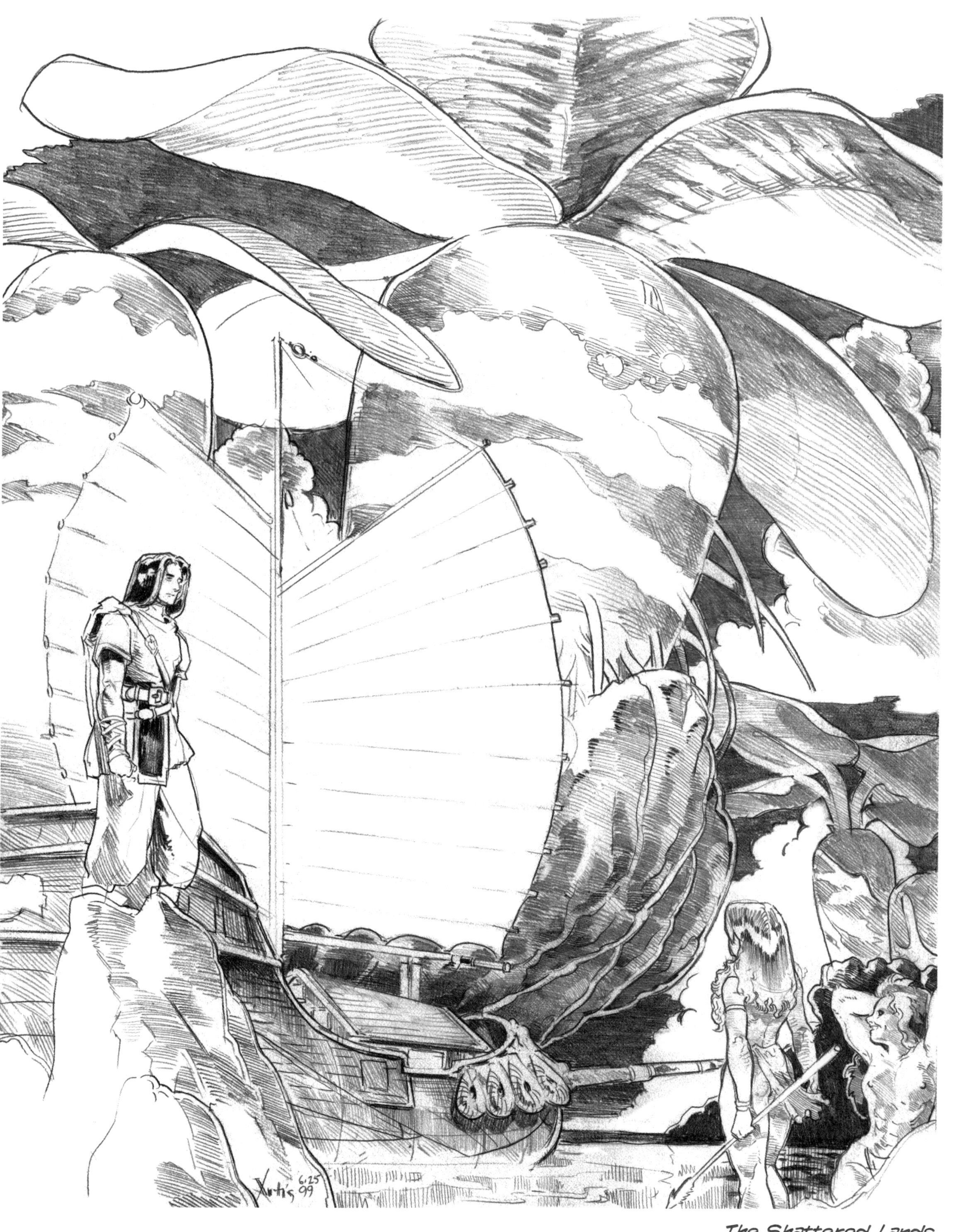

The Shattered Lands

A fantasy environment humans share with otter-like humanoids.

Ex Libris

This is one of the those otter-girls who lives in the land of the big turnips.

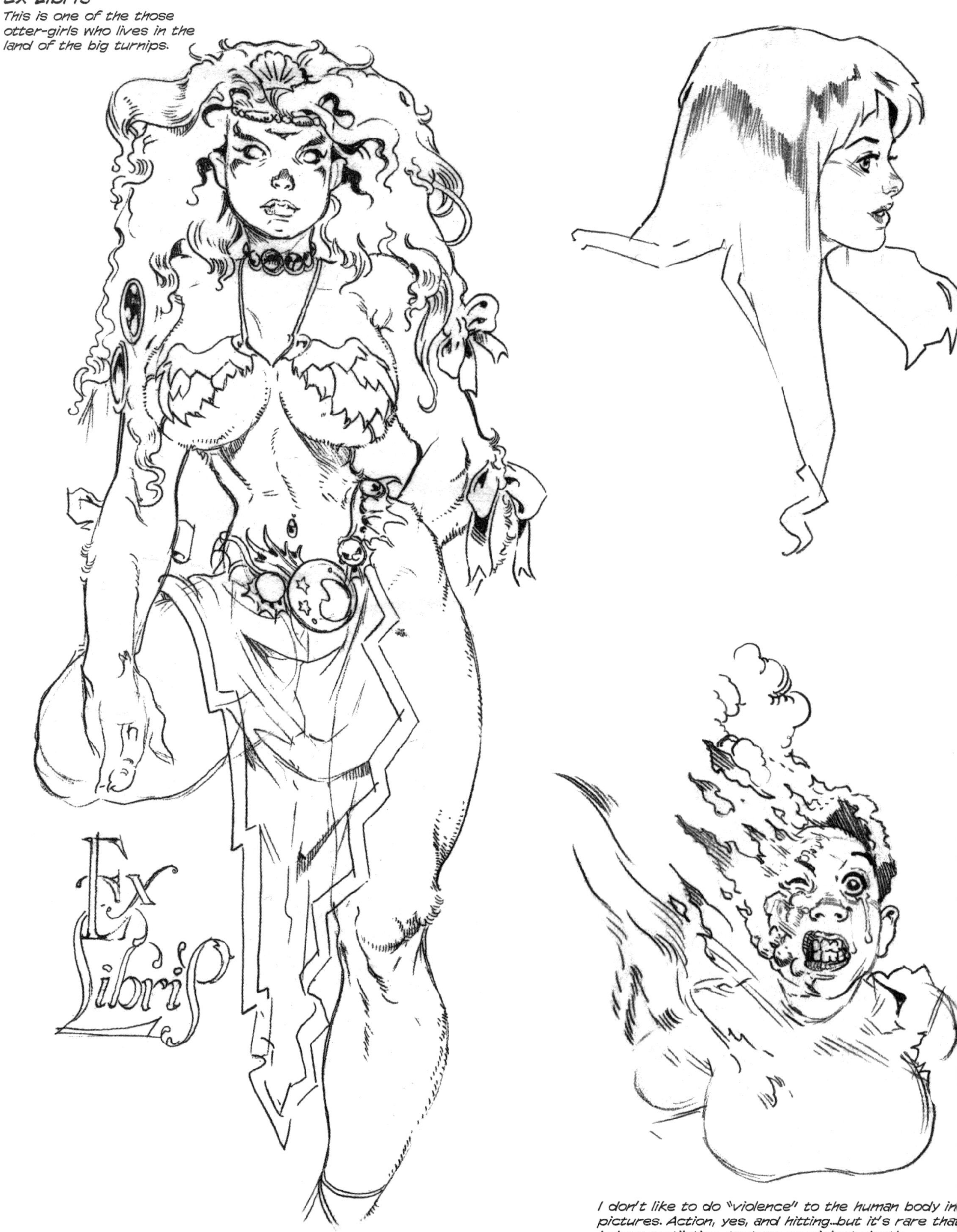

I don't like to do "violence" to the human body in pictures. Action, yes, and hitting...but it's rare that I draw mutilation, torture or violent death.

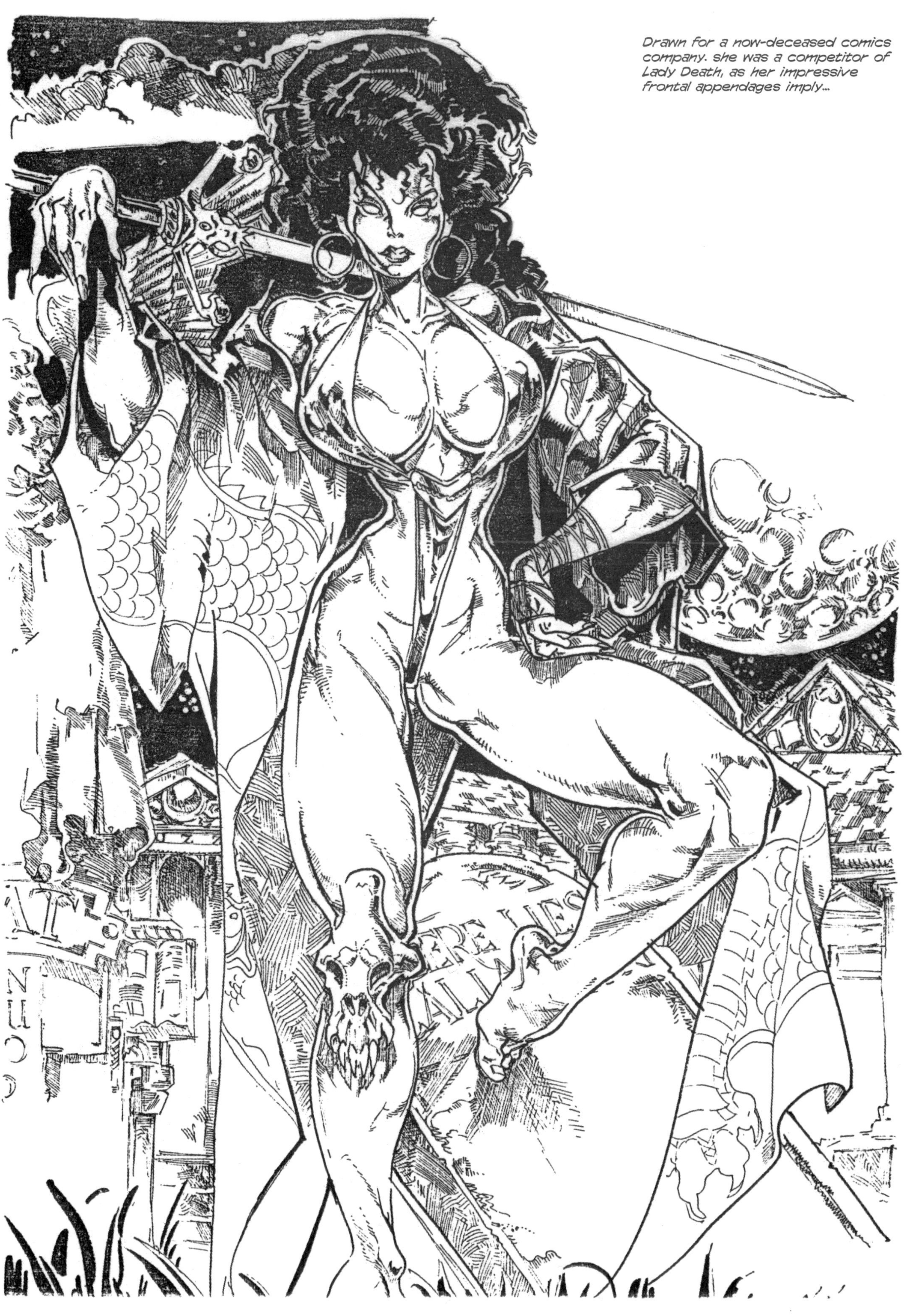

Drawn for a now-deceased comics company. she was a competitor of Lady Death, as her impressive frontal appendages imply...

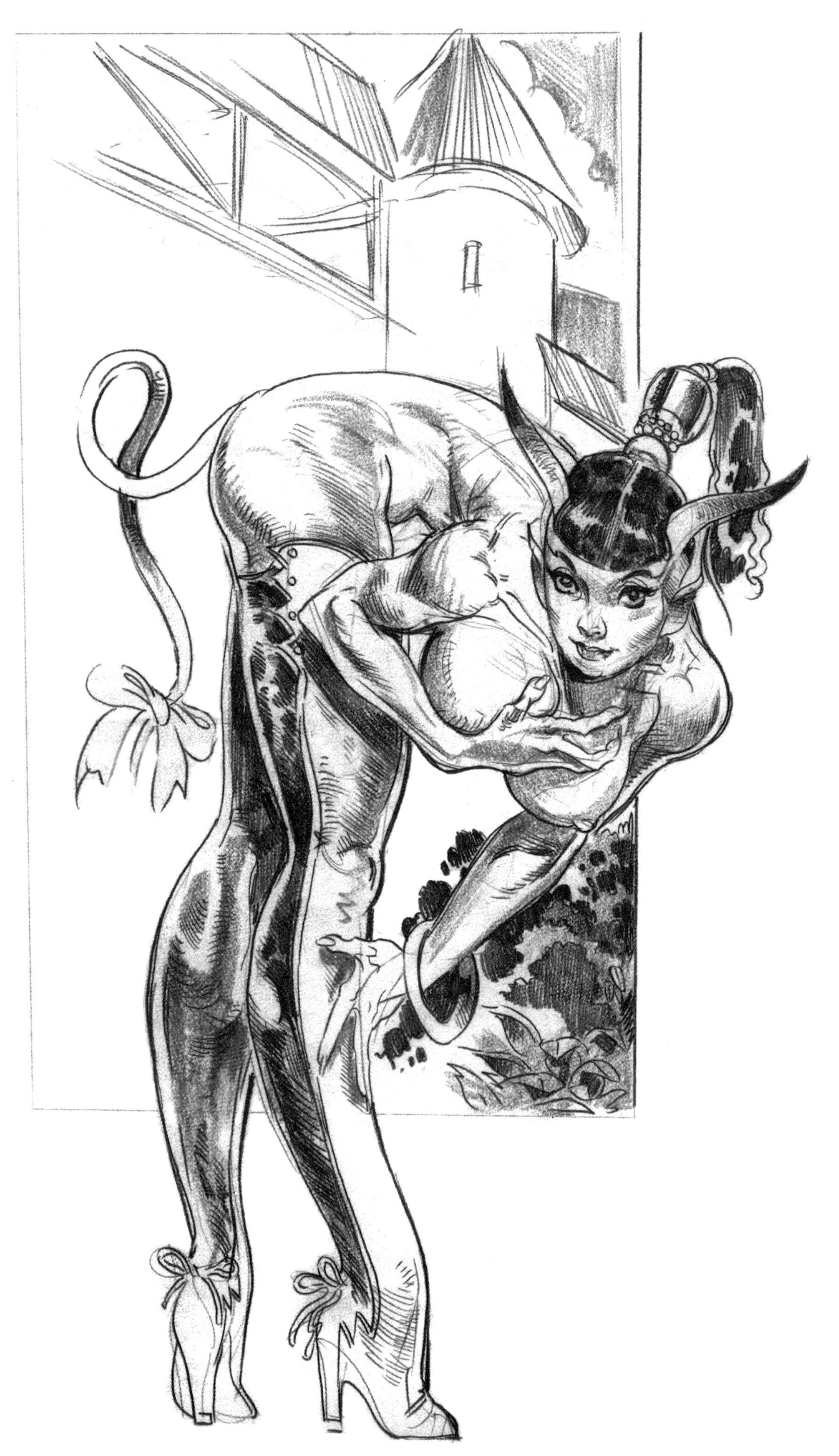

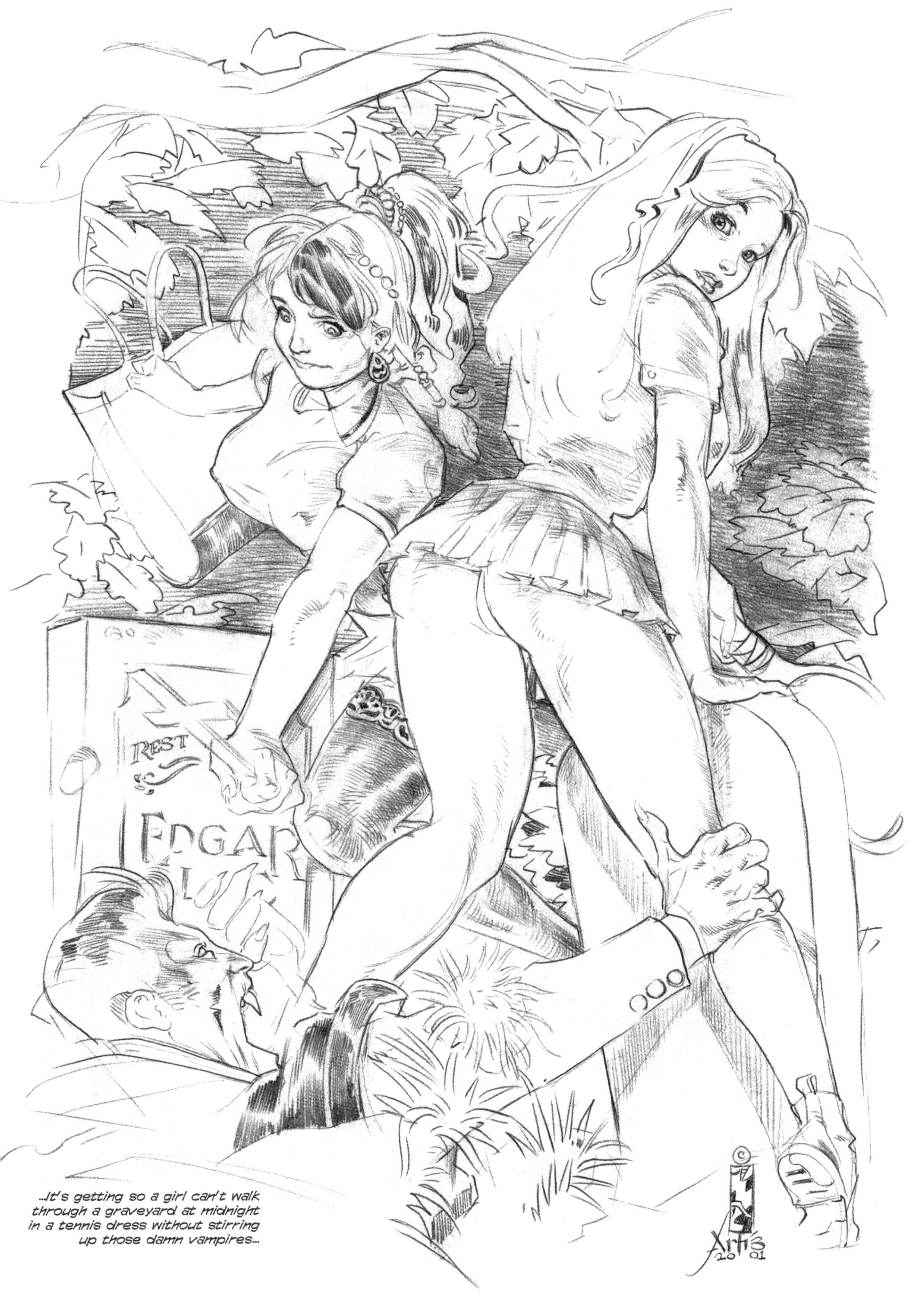

...It's getting so a girl can't walk through a graveyard at midnight in a tennis dress without stirring up those damn vampires...

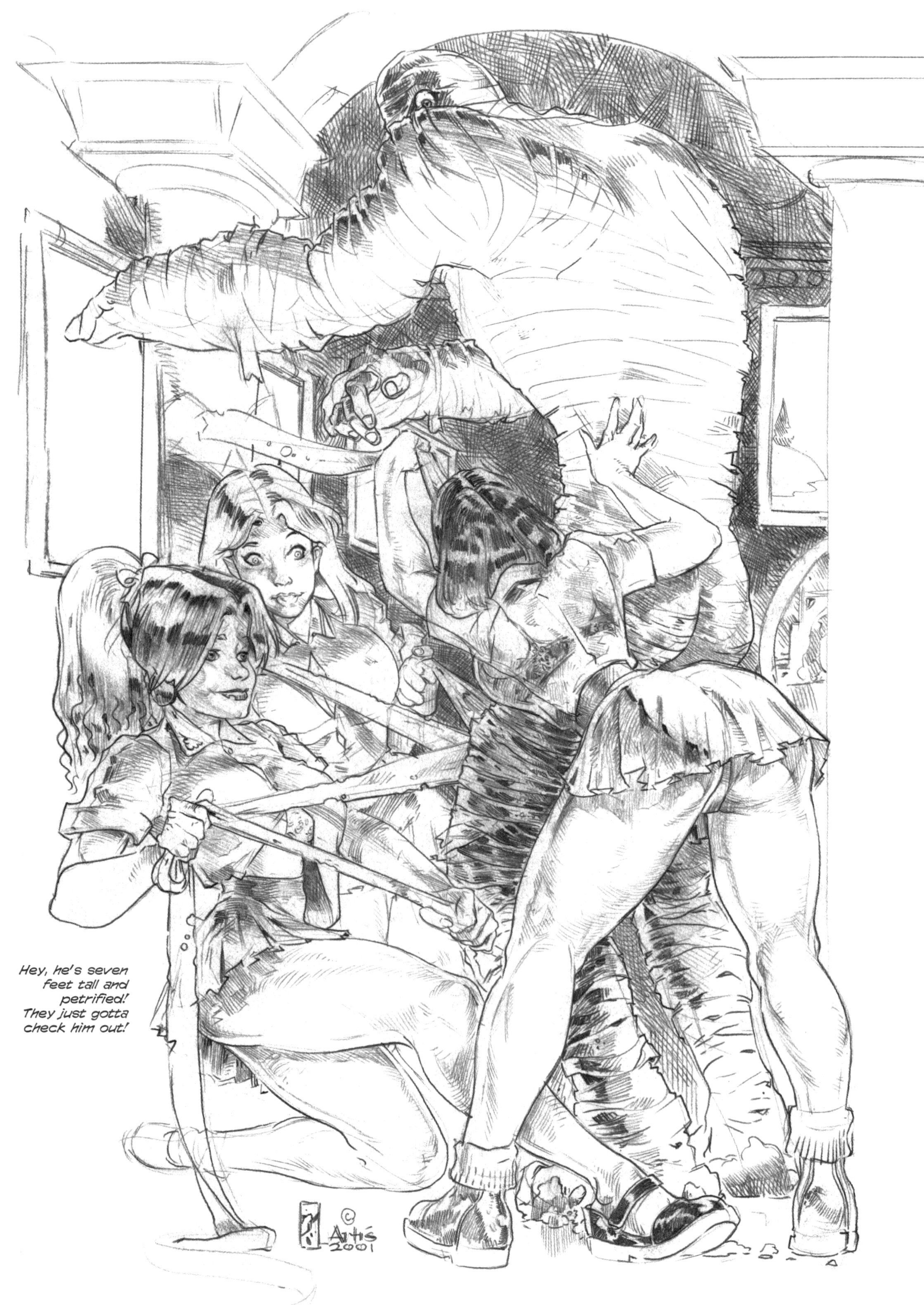

Hey, he's seven feet tall and petrified! They just gotta check him out!

You know, you never see female versions of the biological monsters - no girl unicorns, giants, or werewolves. No girl ogres until "Shreck" for that matter. so I draw 'em.

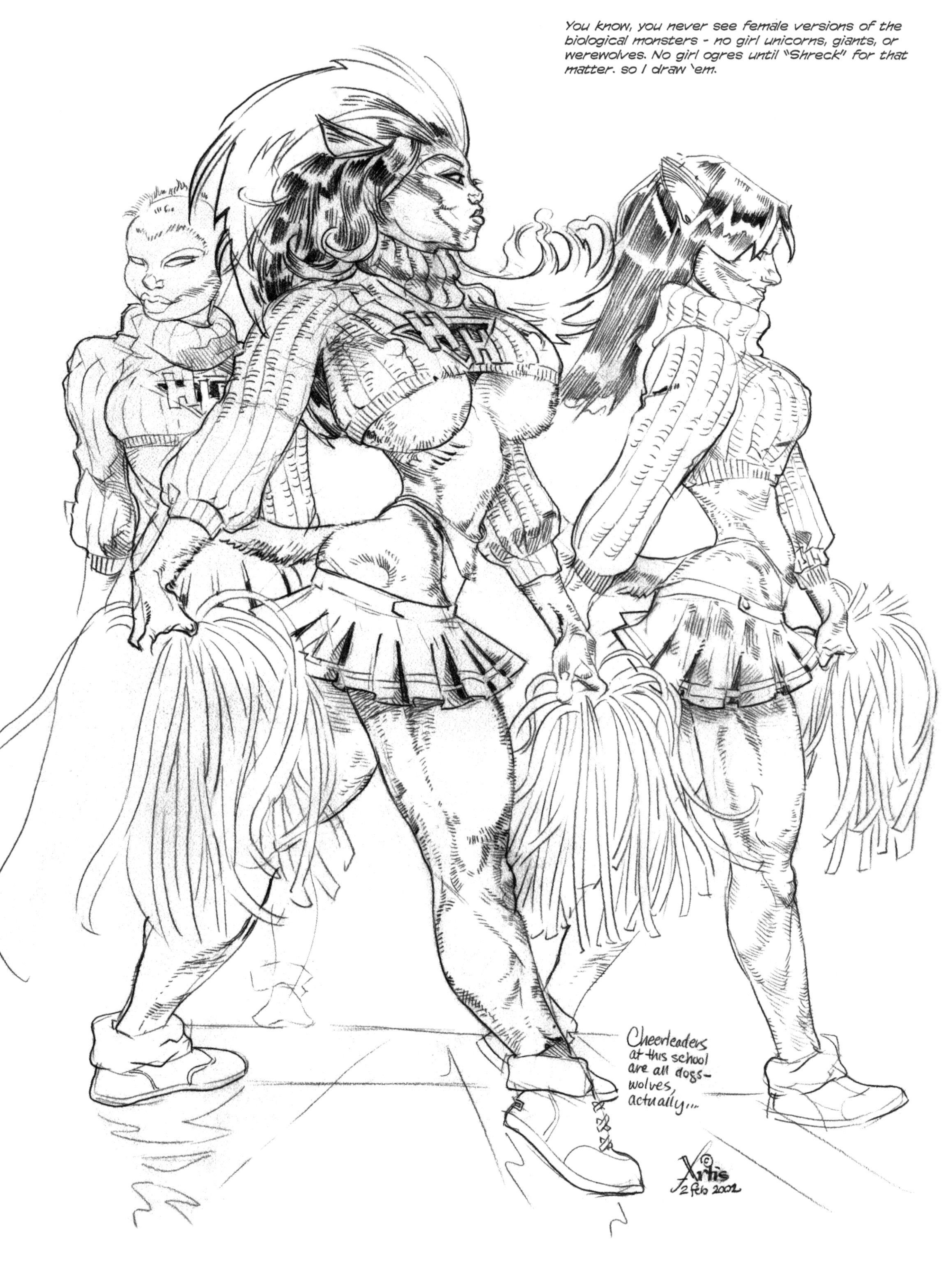

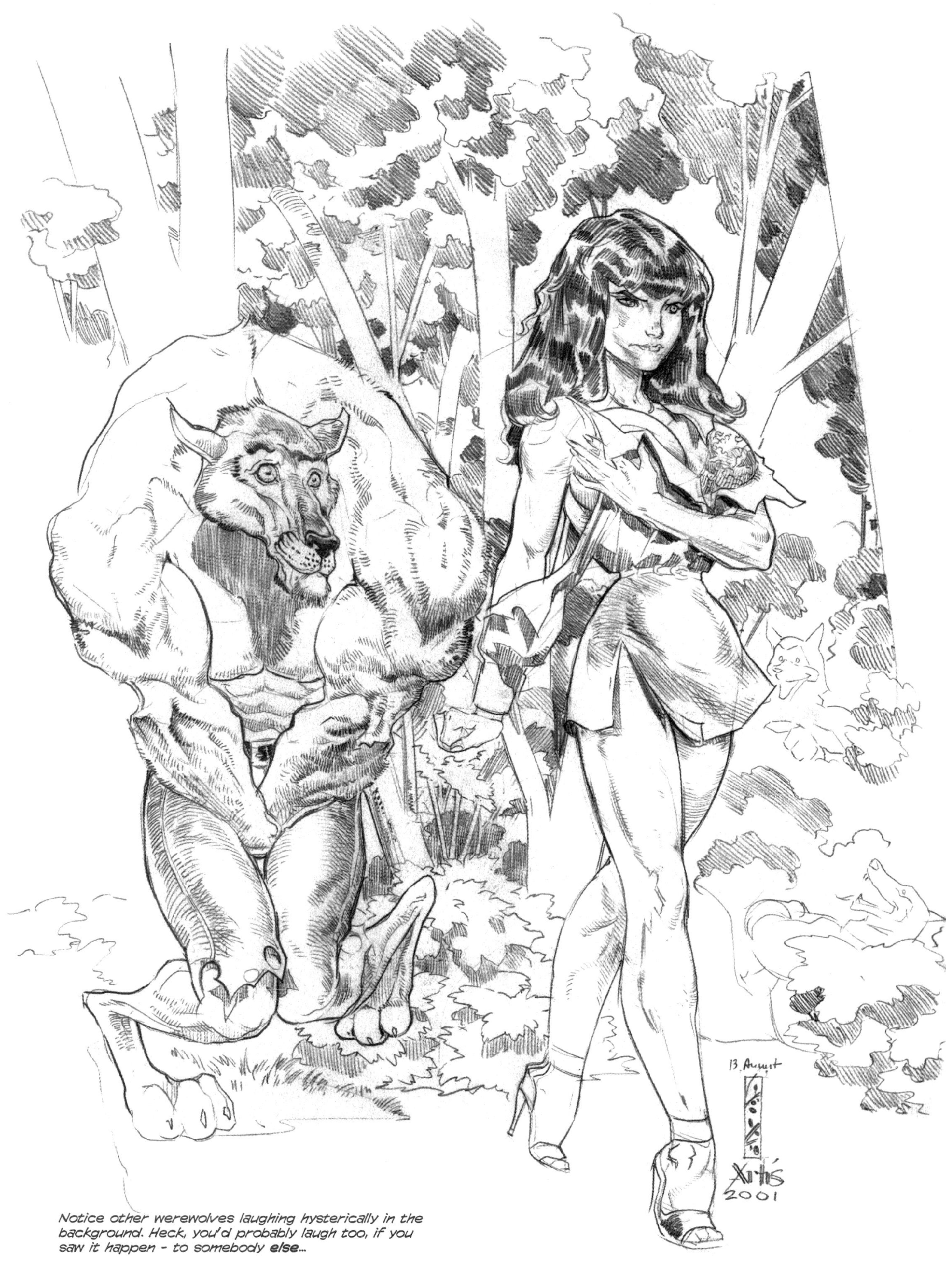

*Notice other werewolves laughing hysterically in the background. Heck, you'd probably laugh too, if you saw it happen - to somebody **else**...*

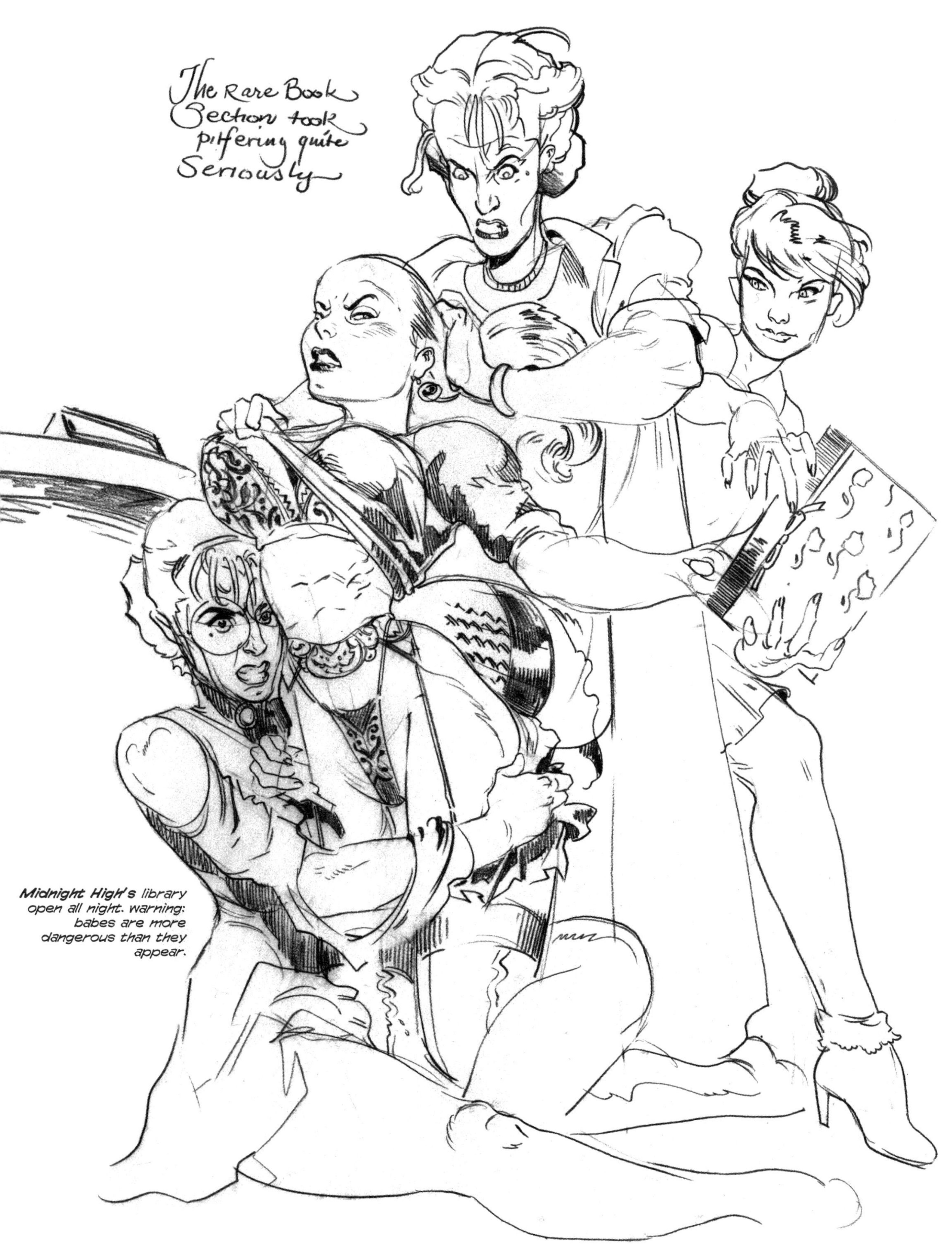

Midnight High's *library open all night. warning: babes are more dangerous than they appear.*

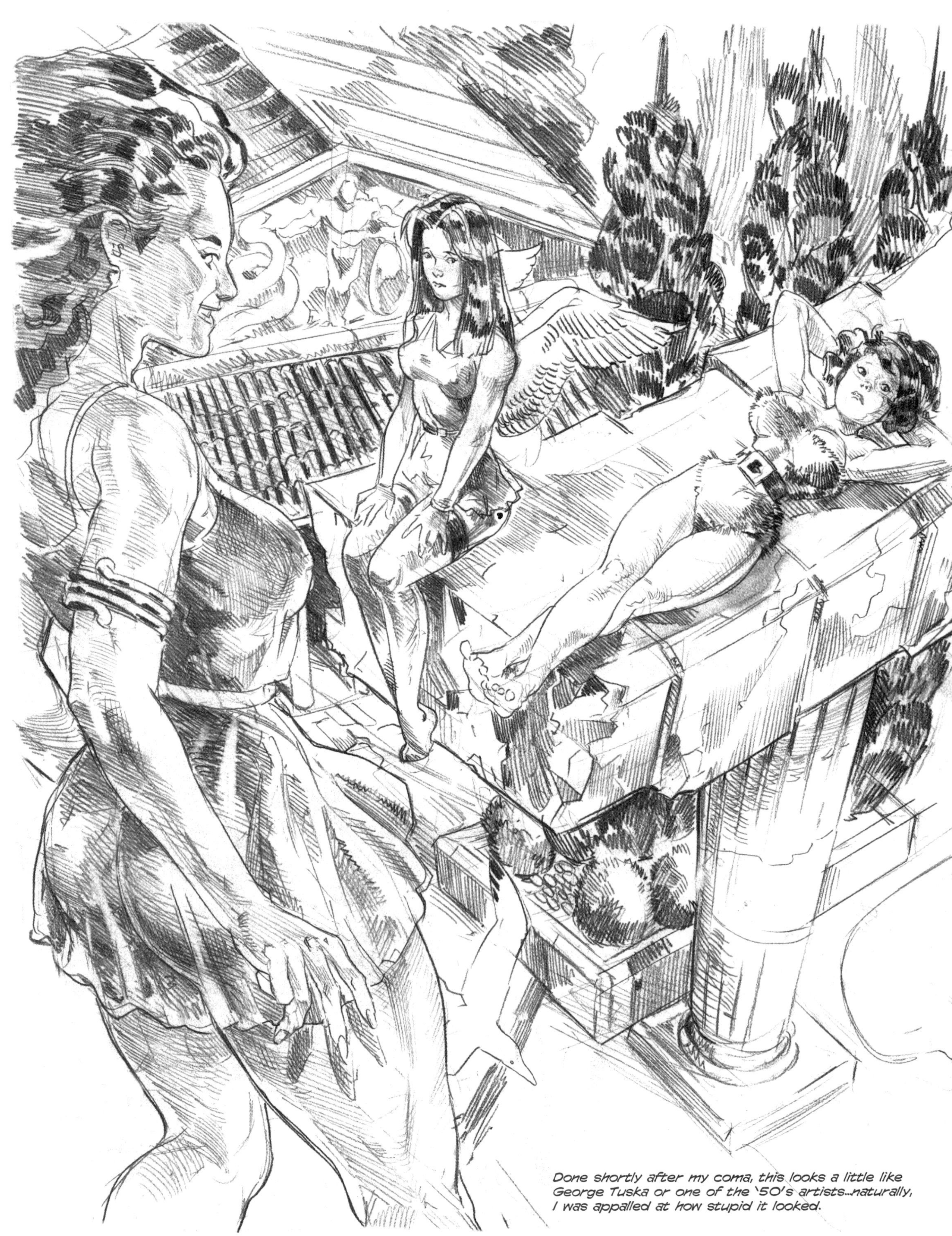

Done shortly after my coma, this looks a little like George Tuska or one of the '50's artists...naturally, I was appalled at how stupid it looked.

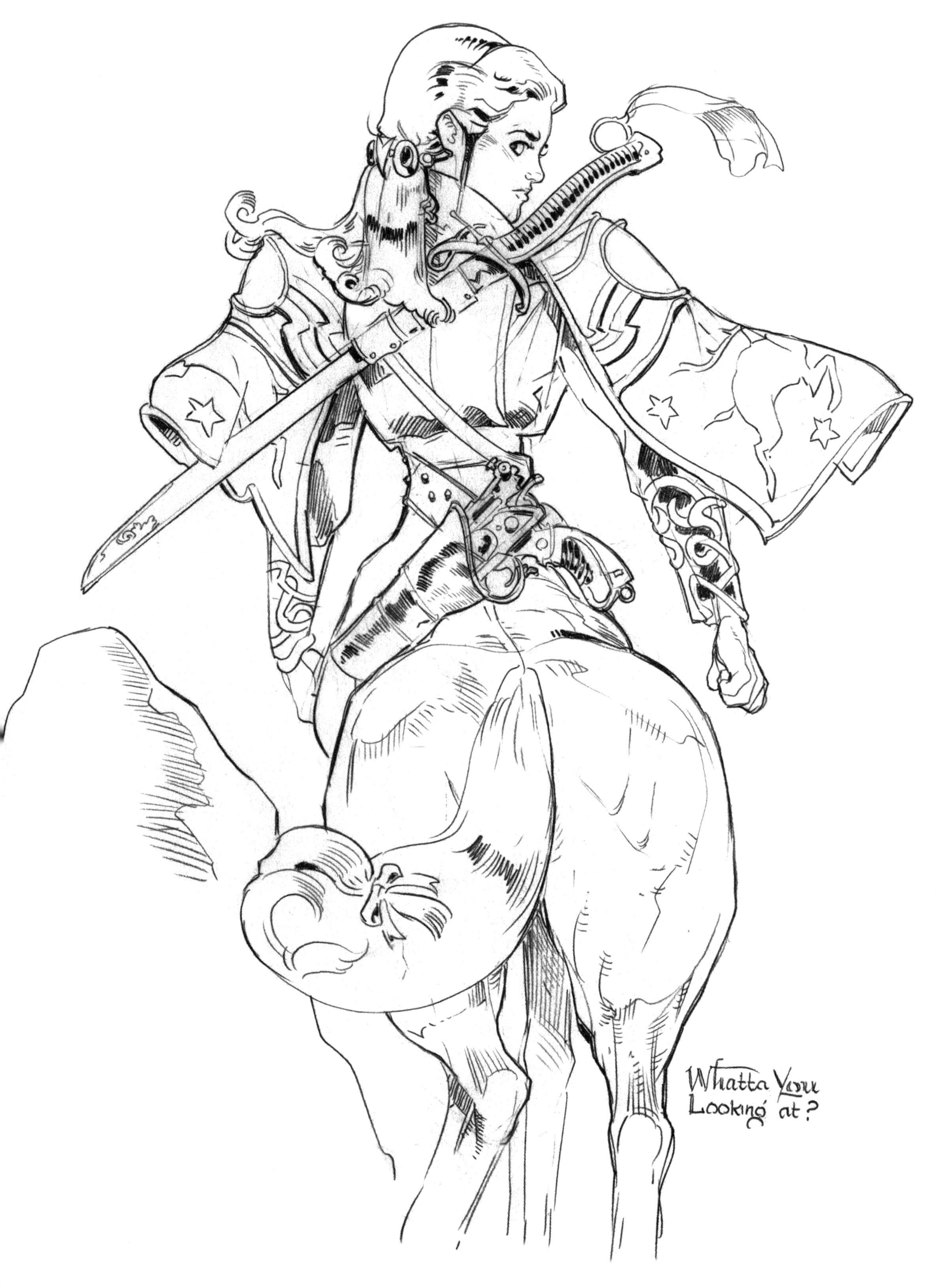
Whatta You
Looking at?

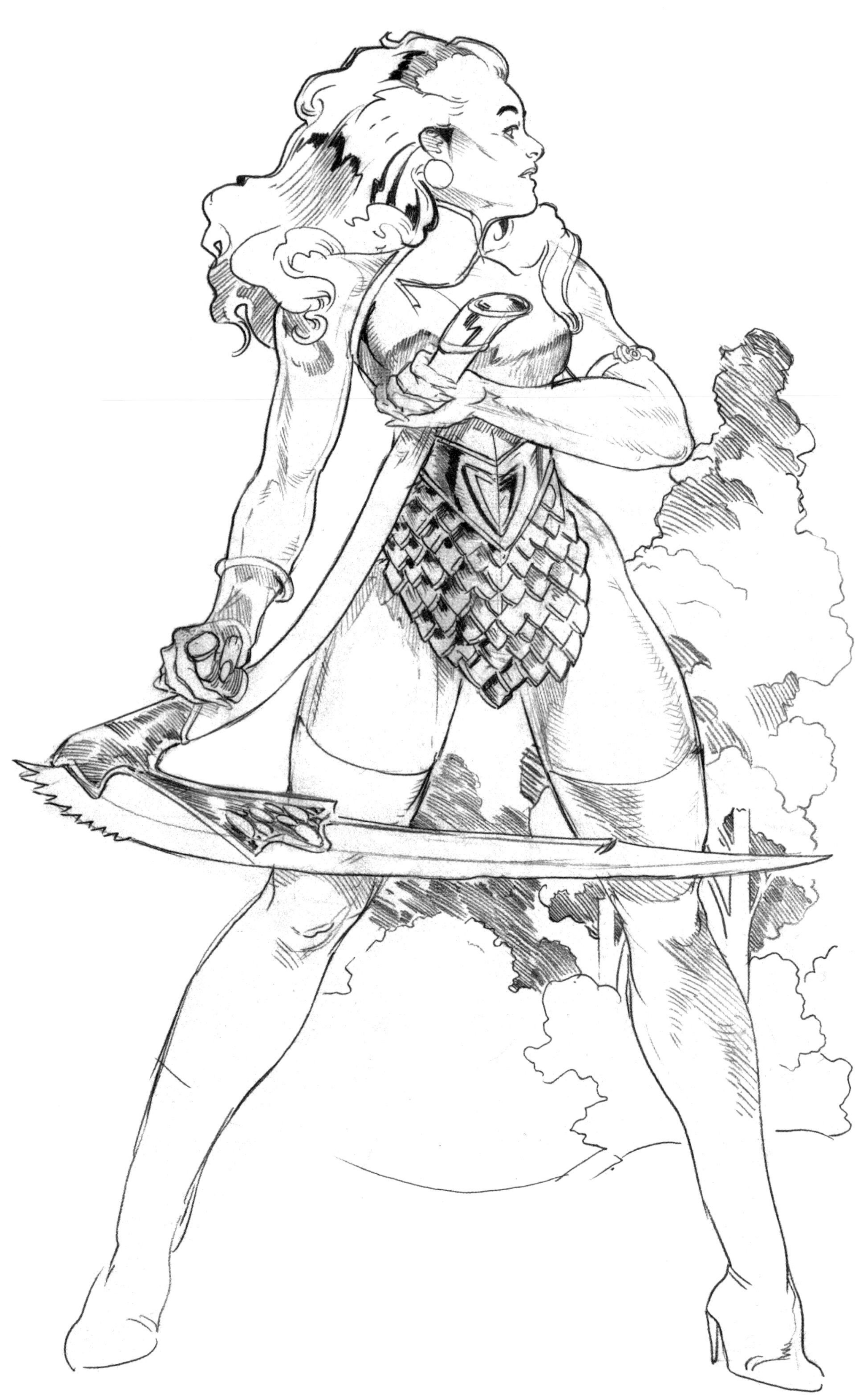

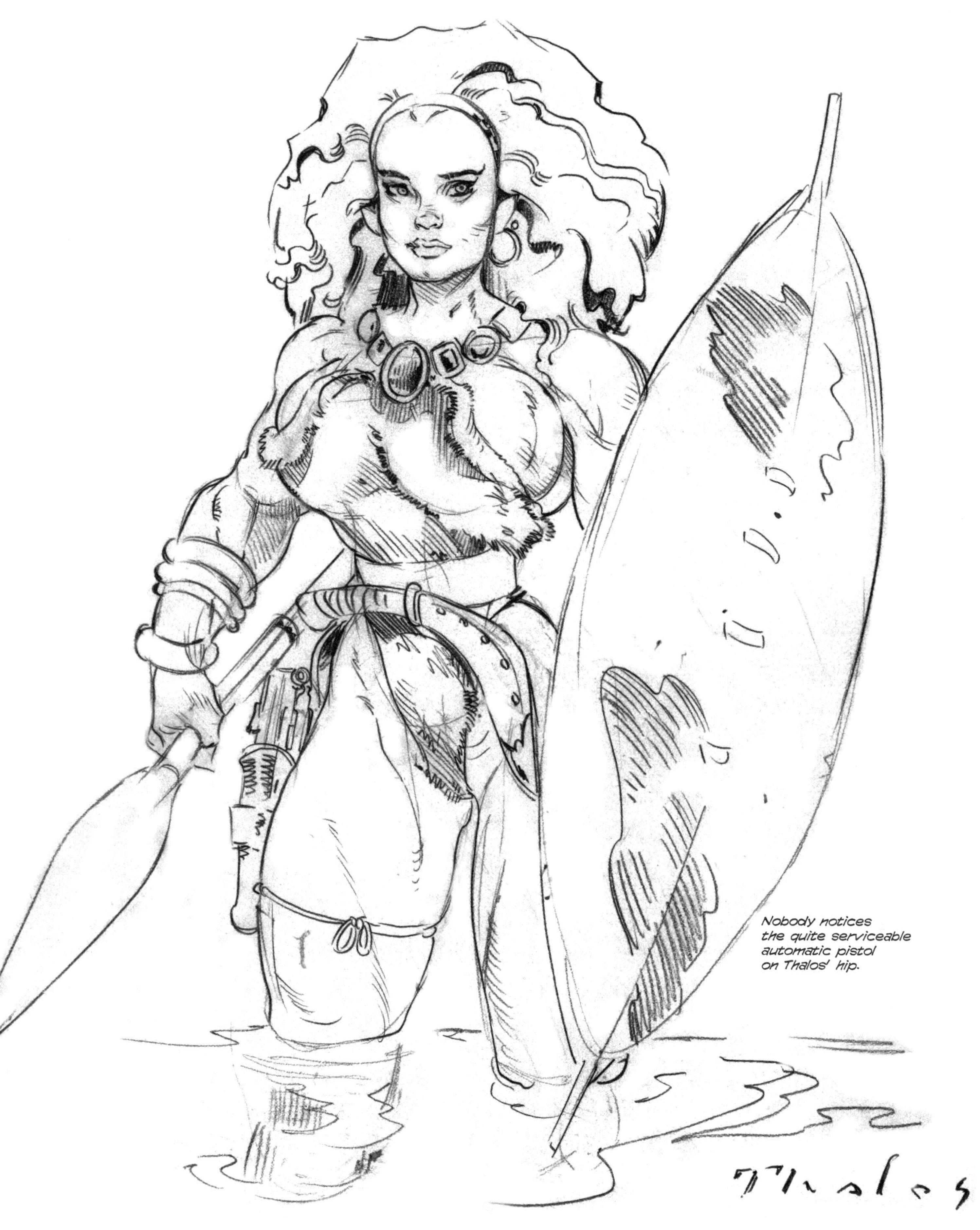

Nobody notices
the quite serviceable
automatic pistol
on Thalos' hip.

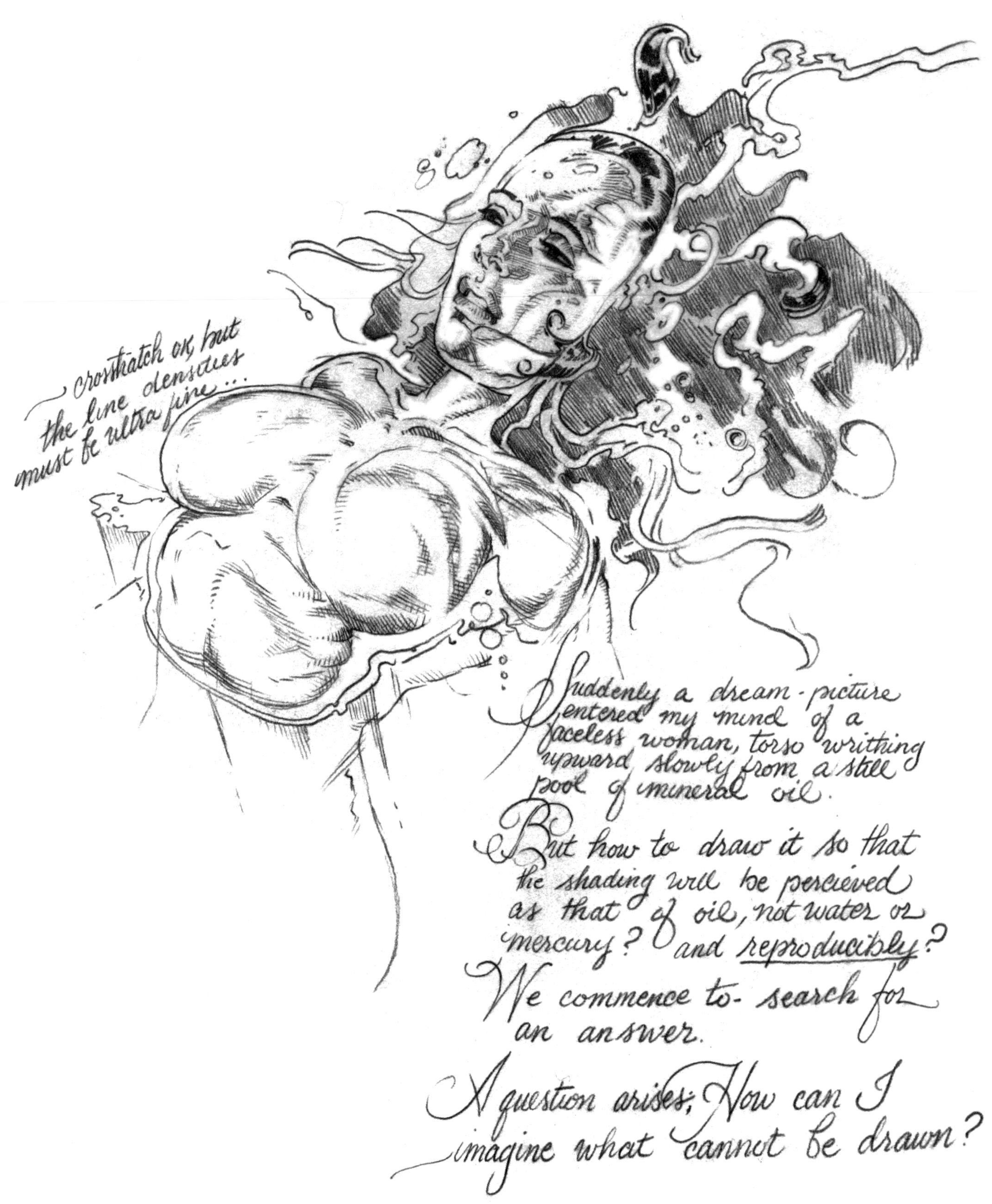
— crosshatch ok, but
the line densities
must be ultra fine...
Suddenly a dream-picture
entered my mind of a
faceless woman, torso writhing
upward slowly from a still
pool of mineral oil.
But how to draw it so that
the shading will be percieved
as that of oil, not water or
mercury? and reproducibly?
We commence to search for
an answer.
A question arises; How can I
imagine what cannot be drawn?

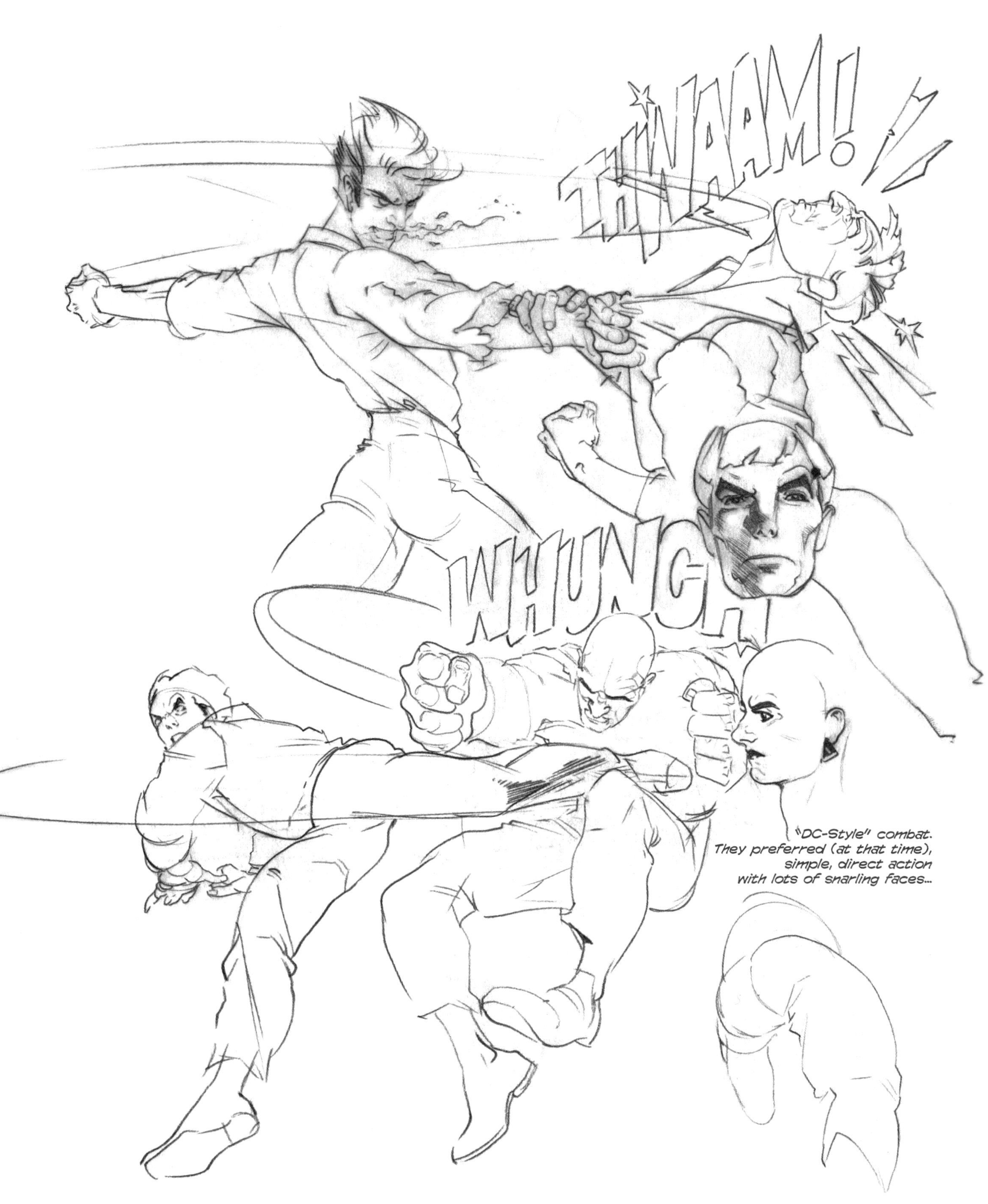

"DC-Style" combat.
They preferred (at that time),
simple, direct action
with lots of snarling faces...

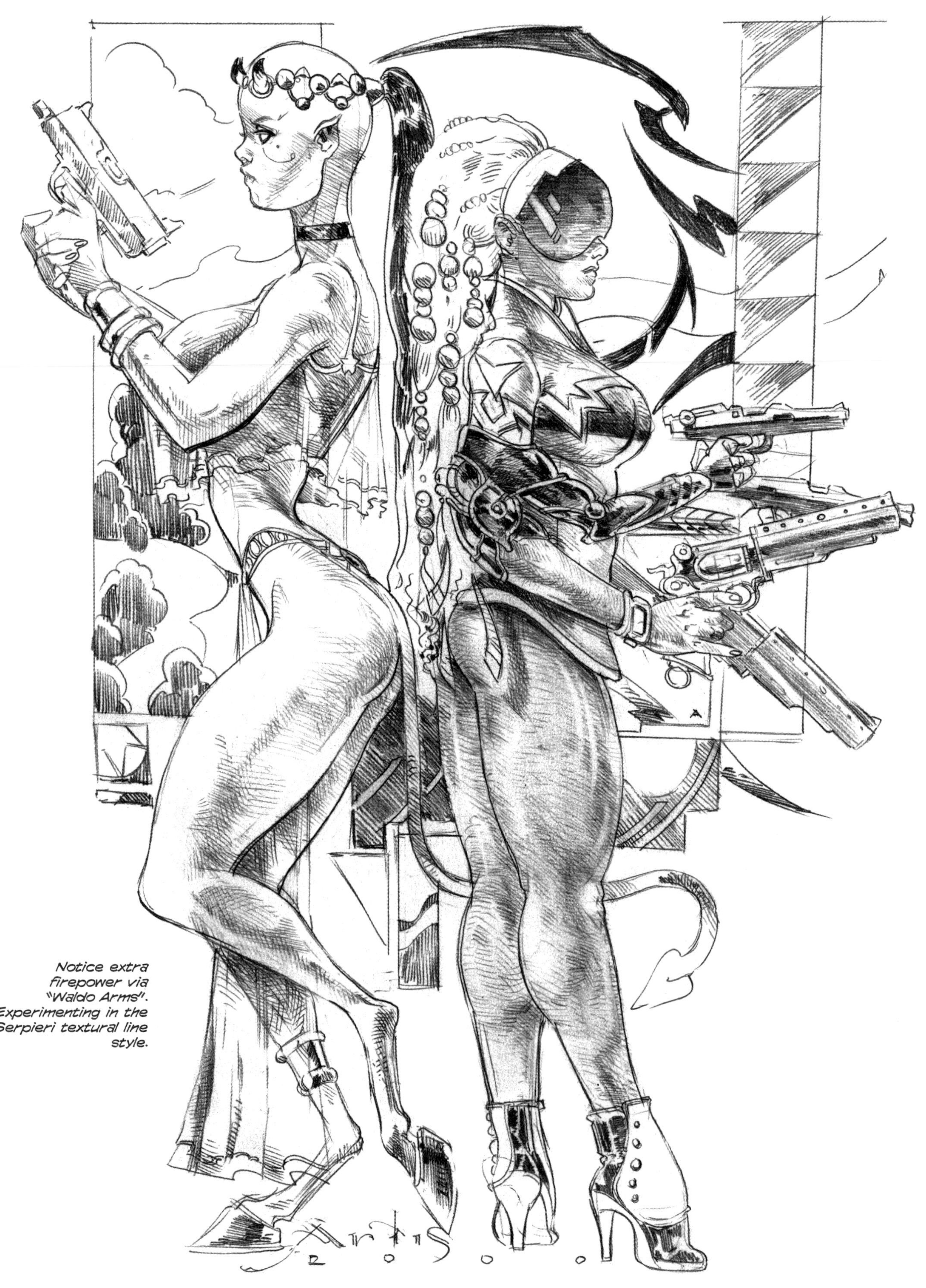

Notice extra firepower via "Waldo Arms". Experimenting in the Serpieri textural line style.

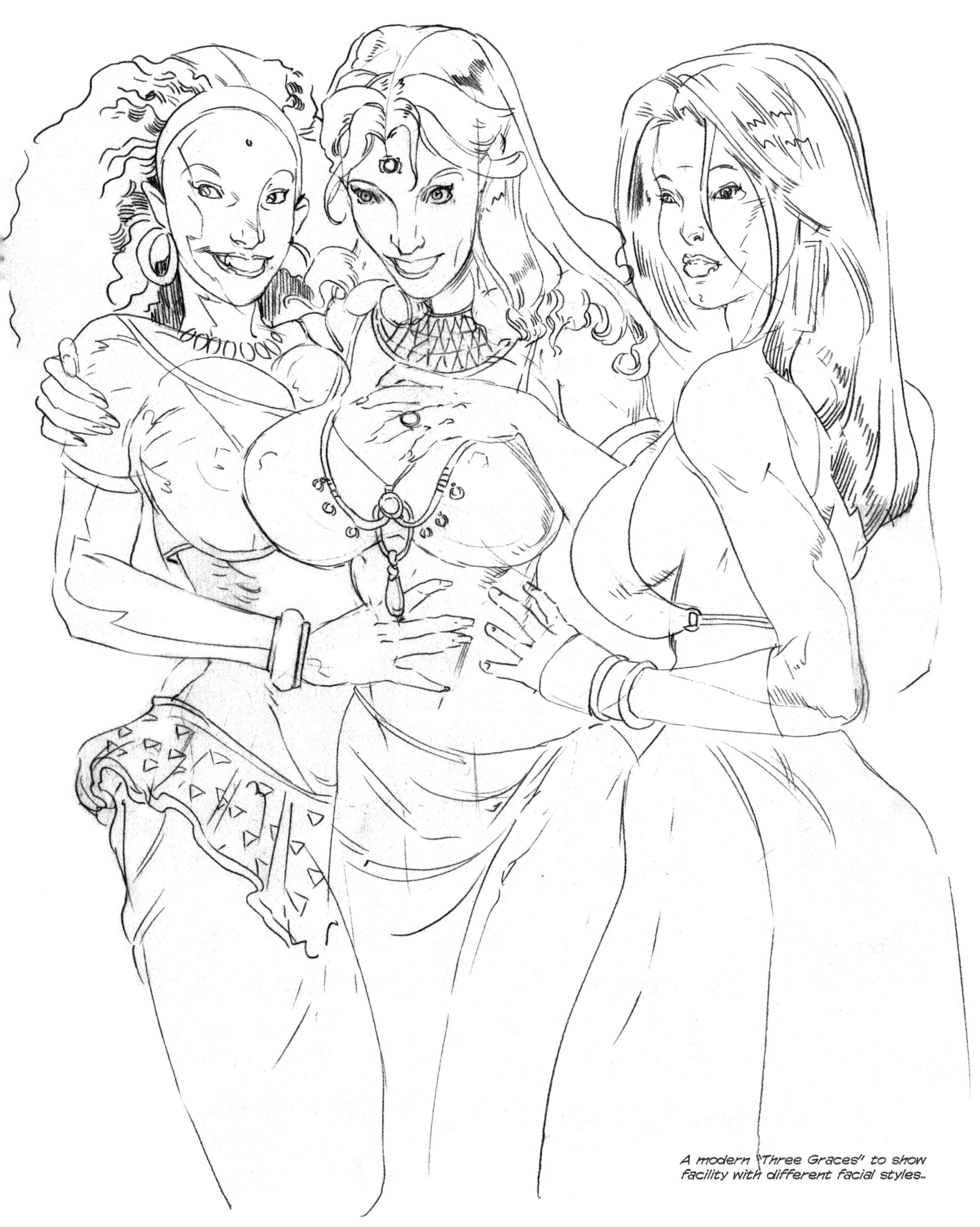

A modern "Three Graces" to show facility with different facial styles..

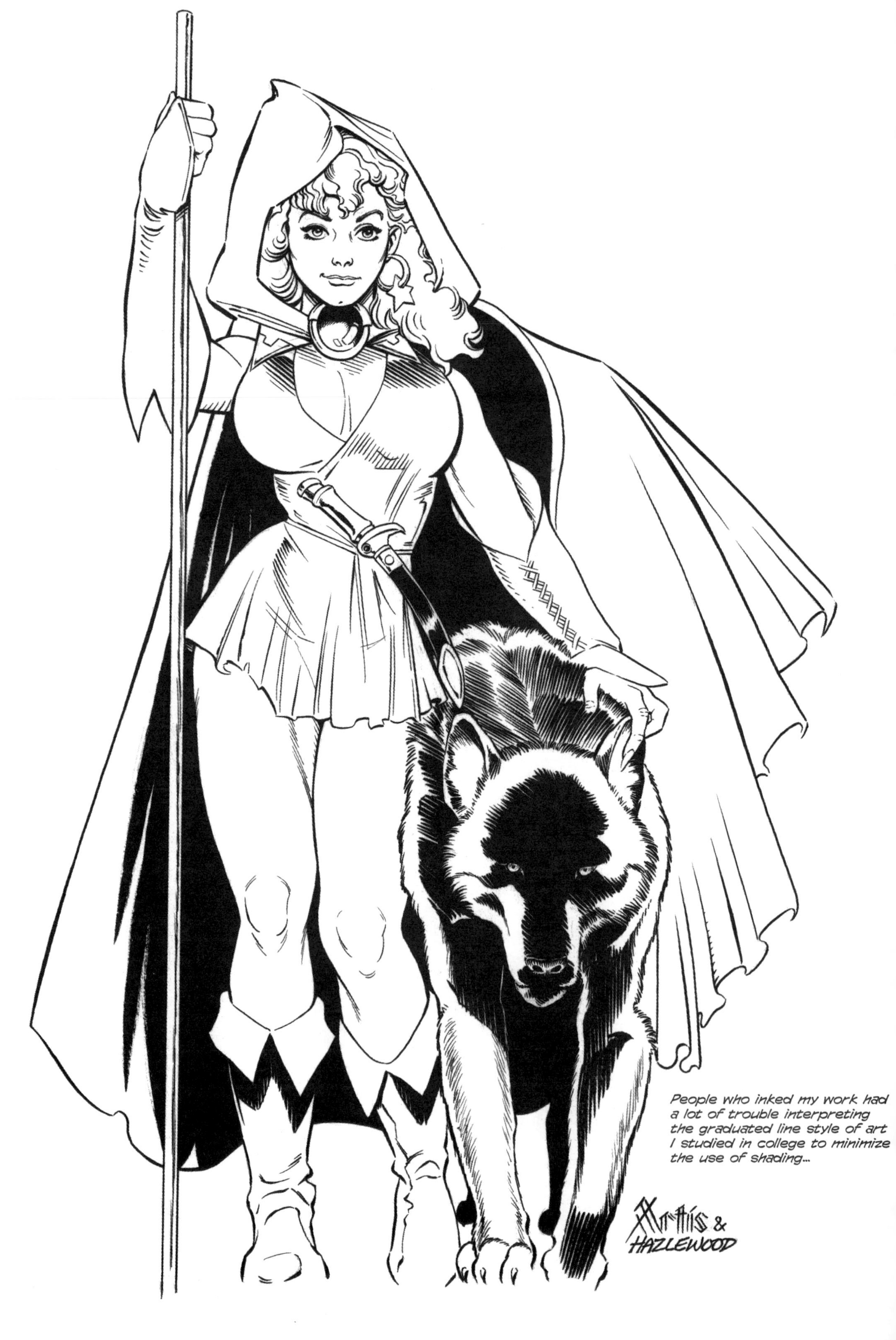

People who inked my work had a lot of trouble interpreting the graduated line style of art I studied in college to minimize the use of shading...

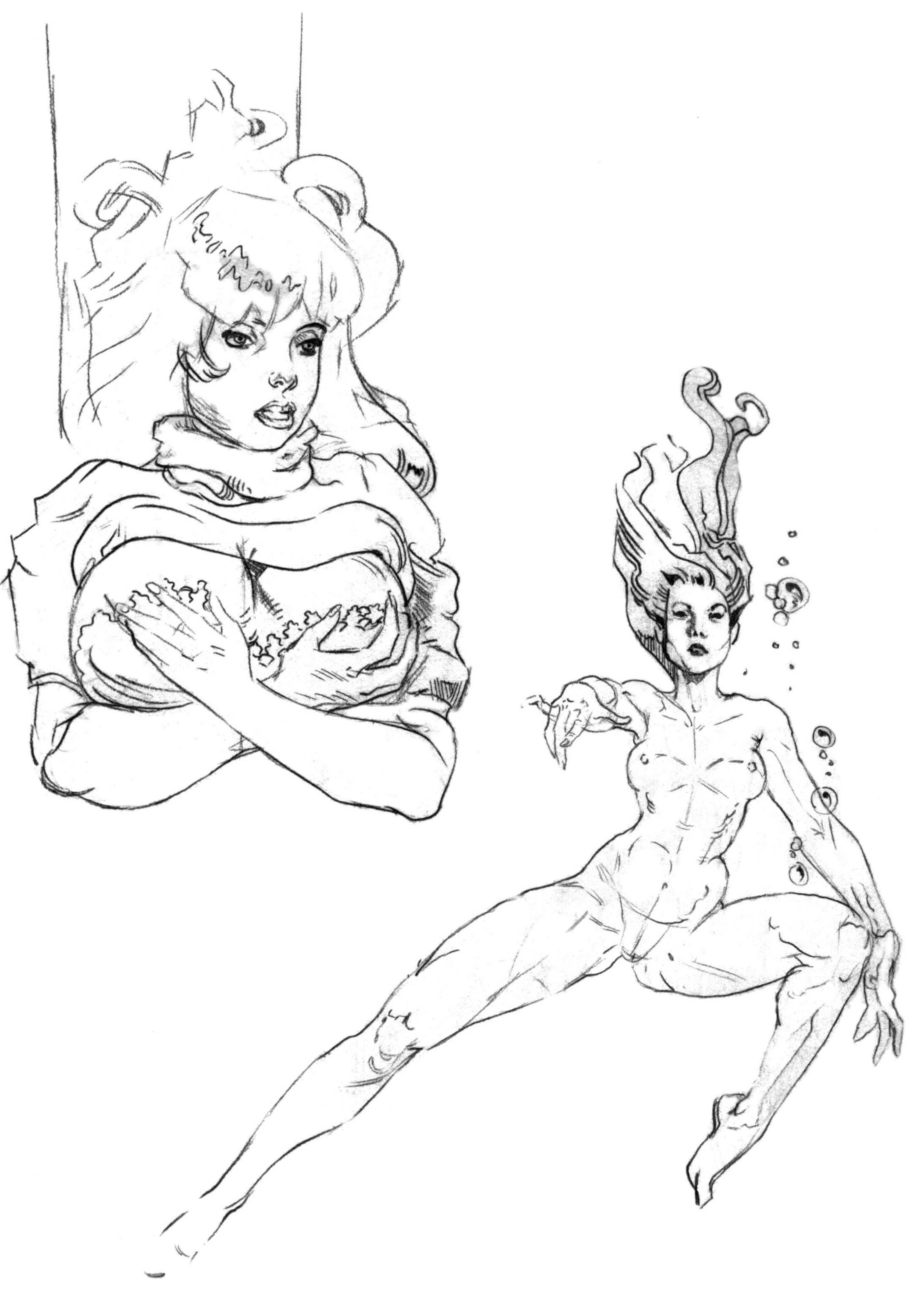

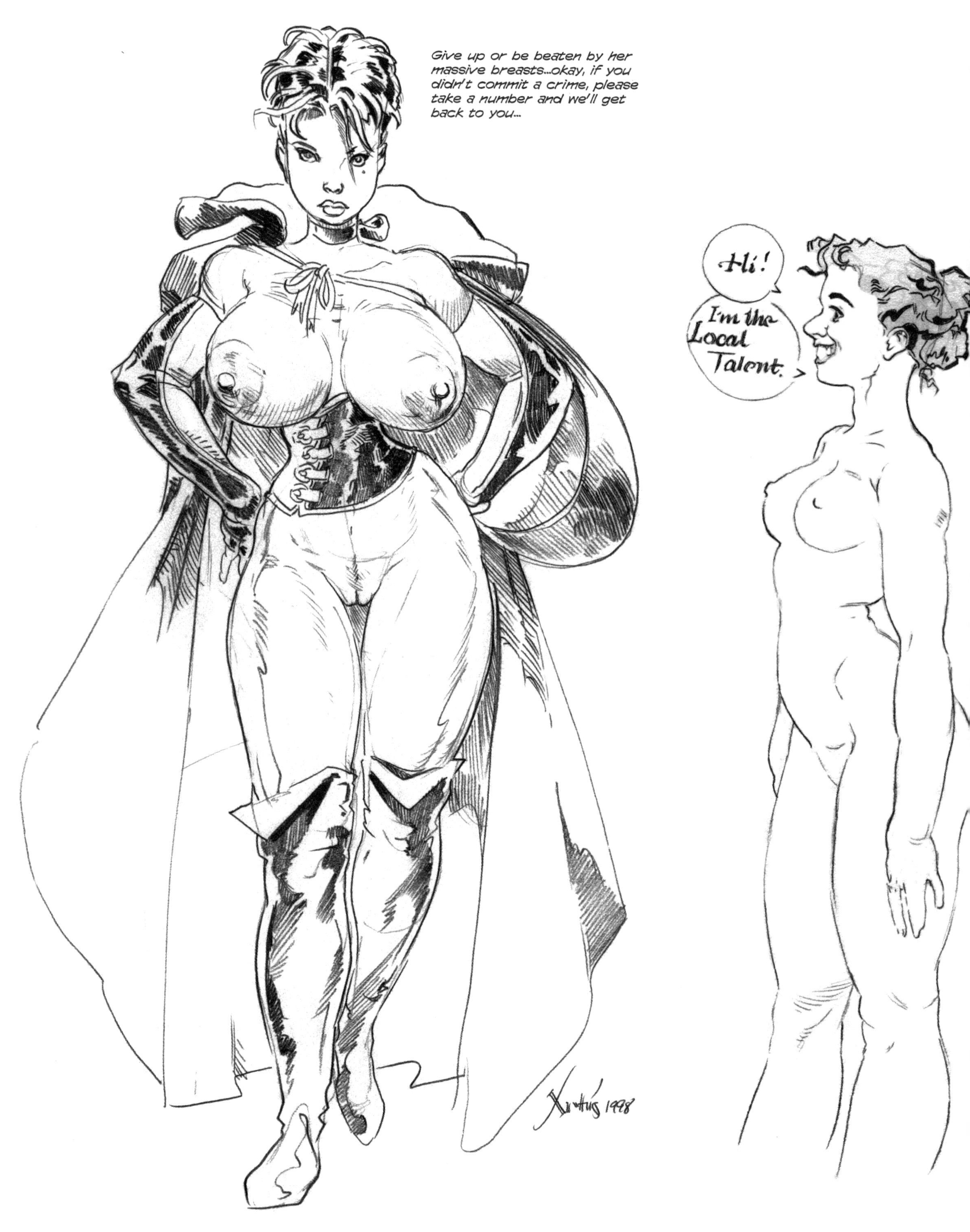
Give up or be beaten by her massive breasts...okay, if you didn't commit a crime, please take a number and we'll get back to you...
Hi!
I'm the Local Talent.

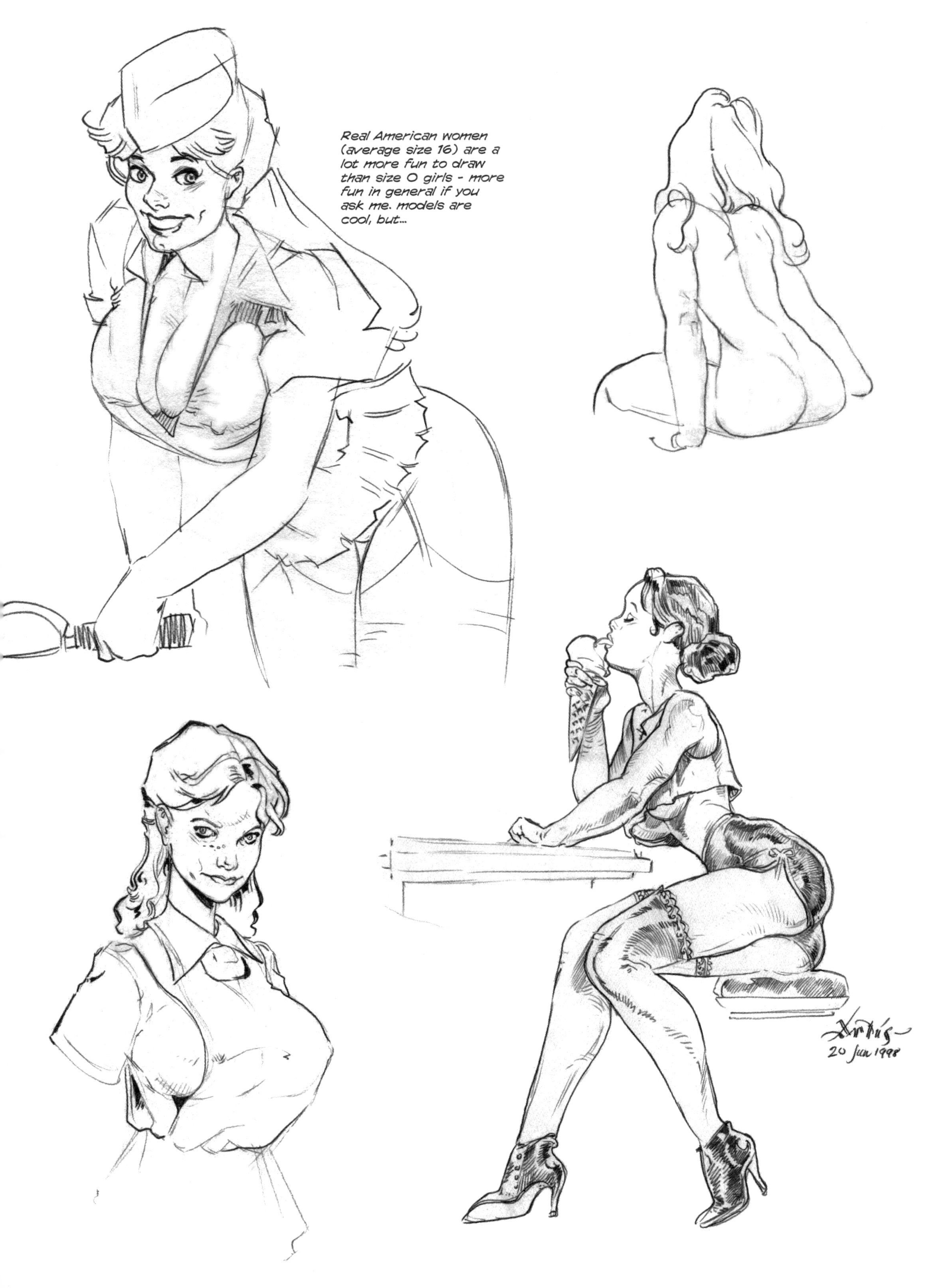
Real American women
(average size 16) are a
lot more fun to draw
than size 0 girls - more
fun in general if you
ask me. models are
cool, but...
20 Jun 1998

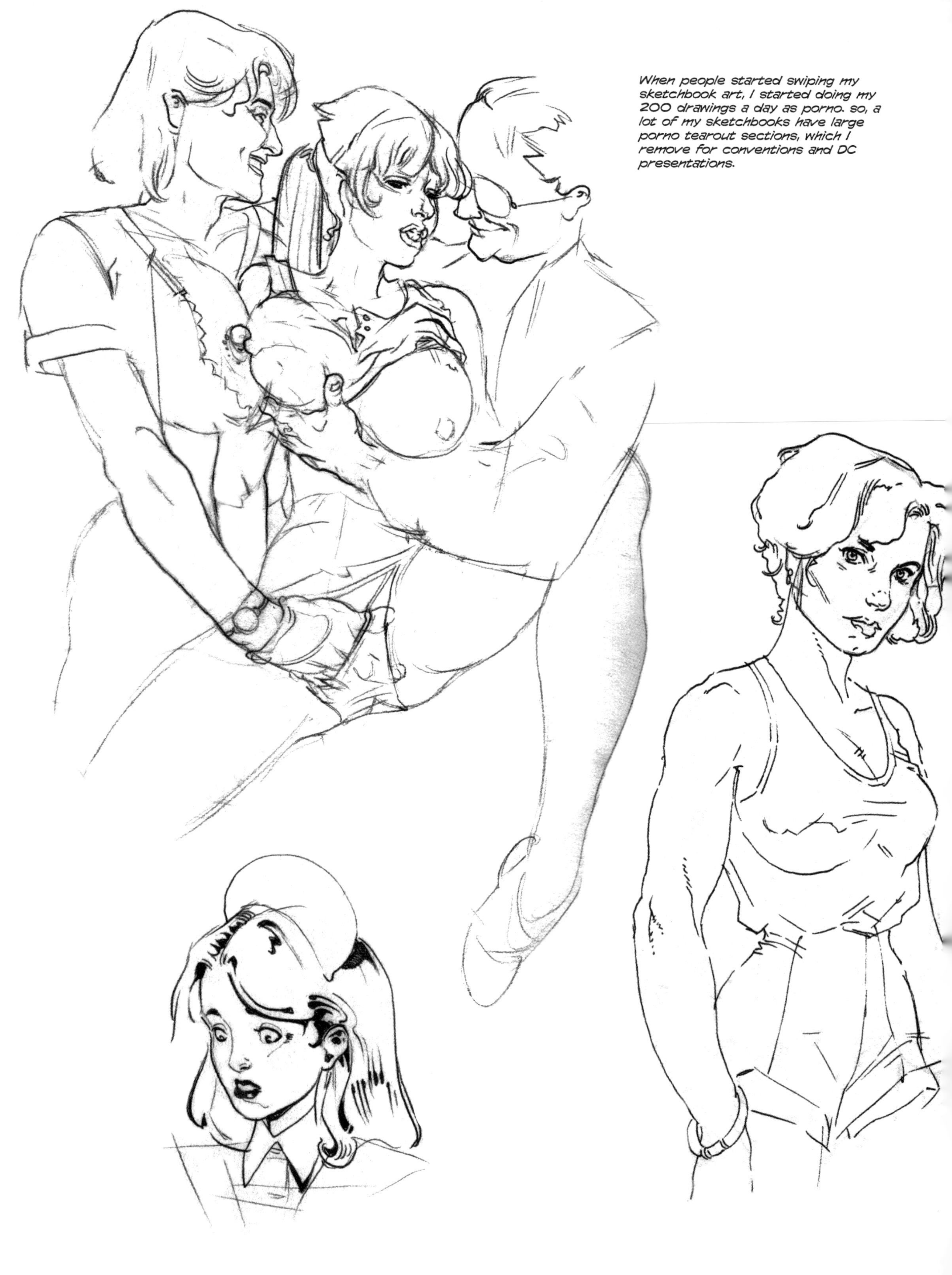

When people started swiping my sketchbook art, I started doing my 200 drawings a day as porno. so, a lot of my sketchbooks have large porno tearout sections, which I remove for conventions and DC presentations.

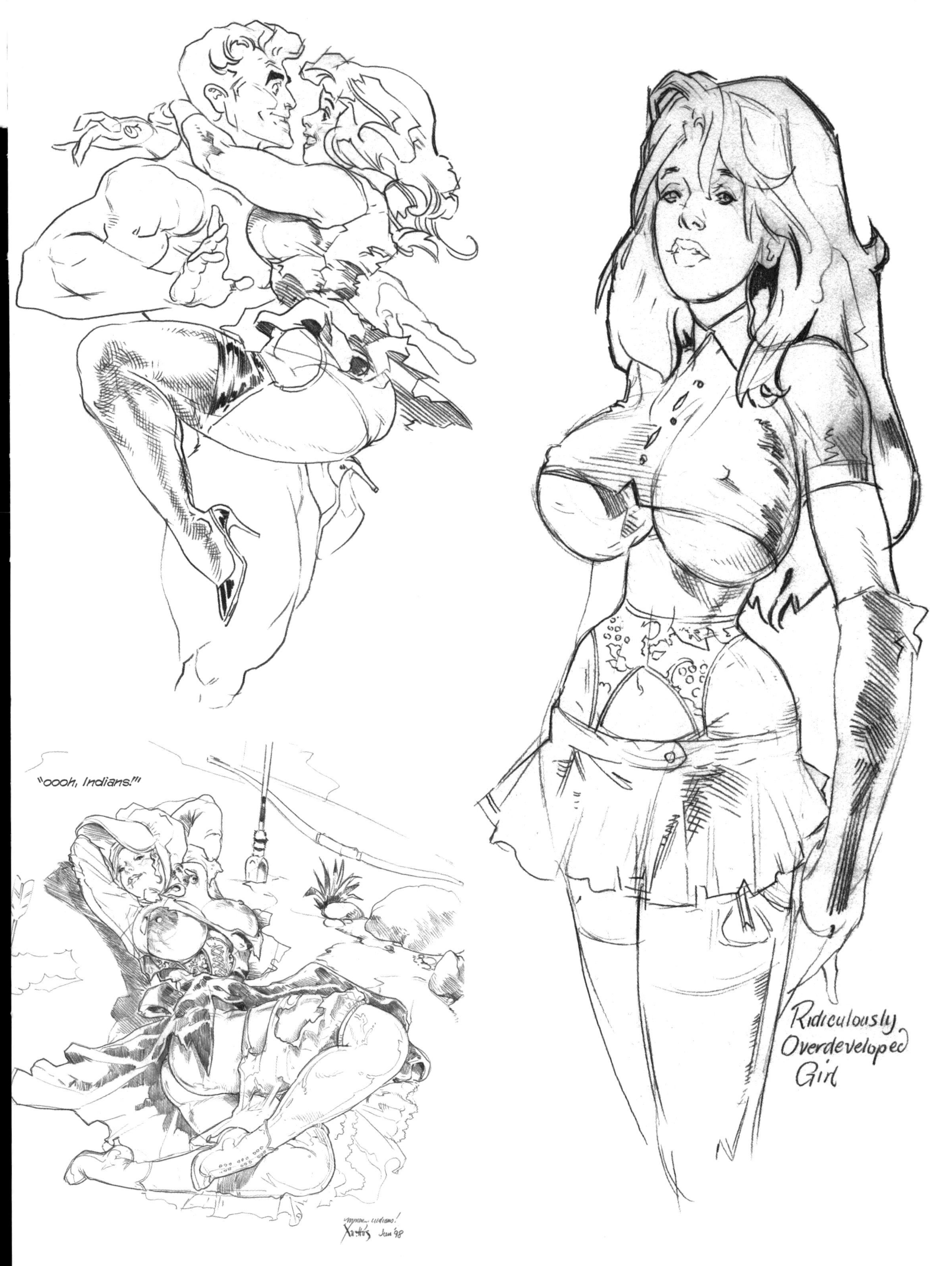
"oooh, Indians!"
Jun '98
Ridiculously Overdeveloped Girl

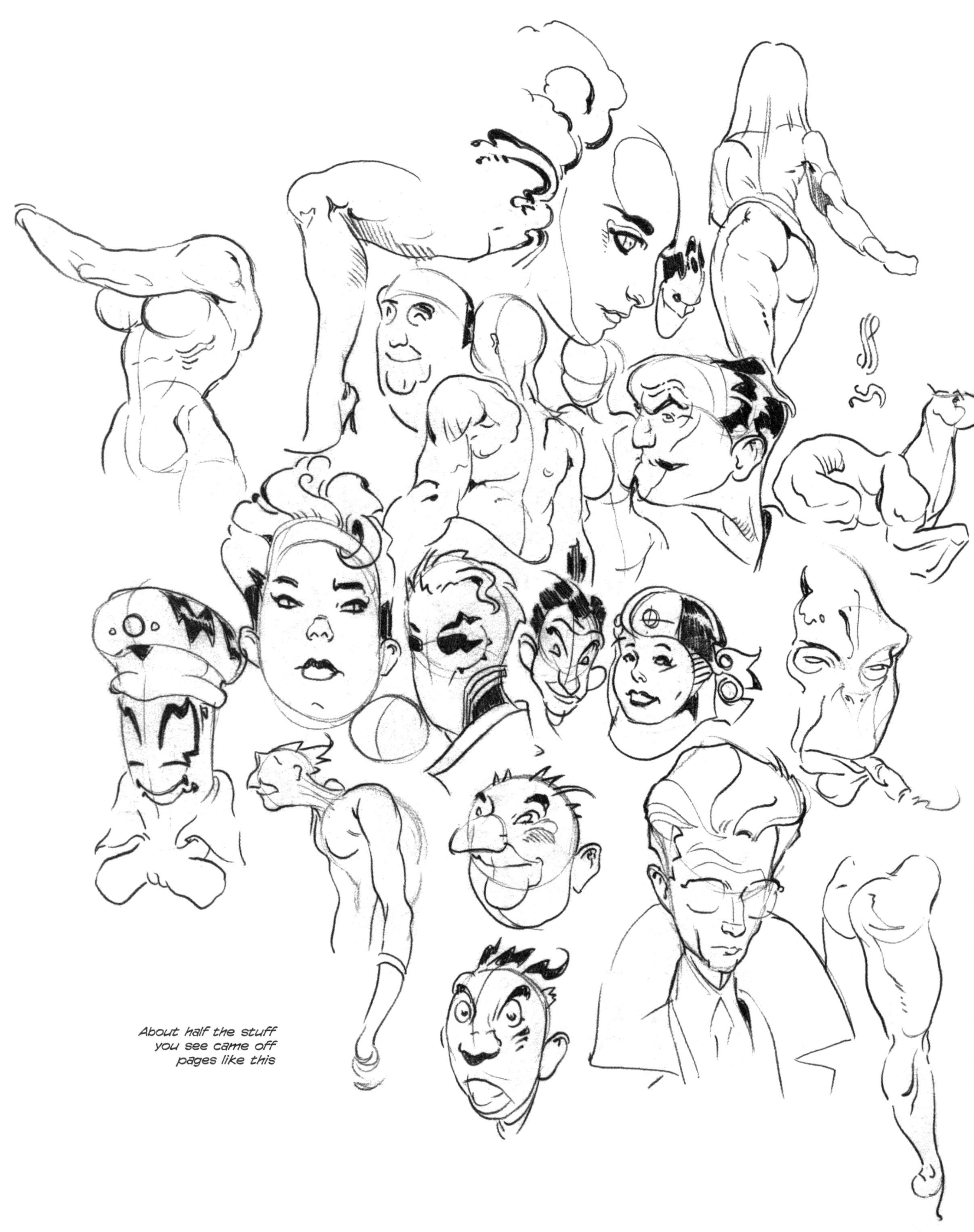

About half the stuff
you see came off
pages like this

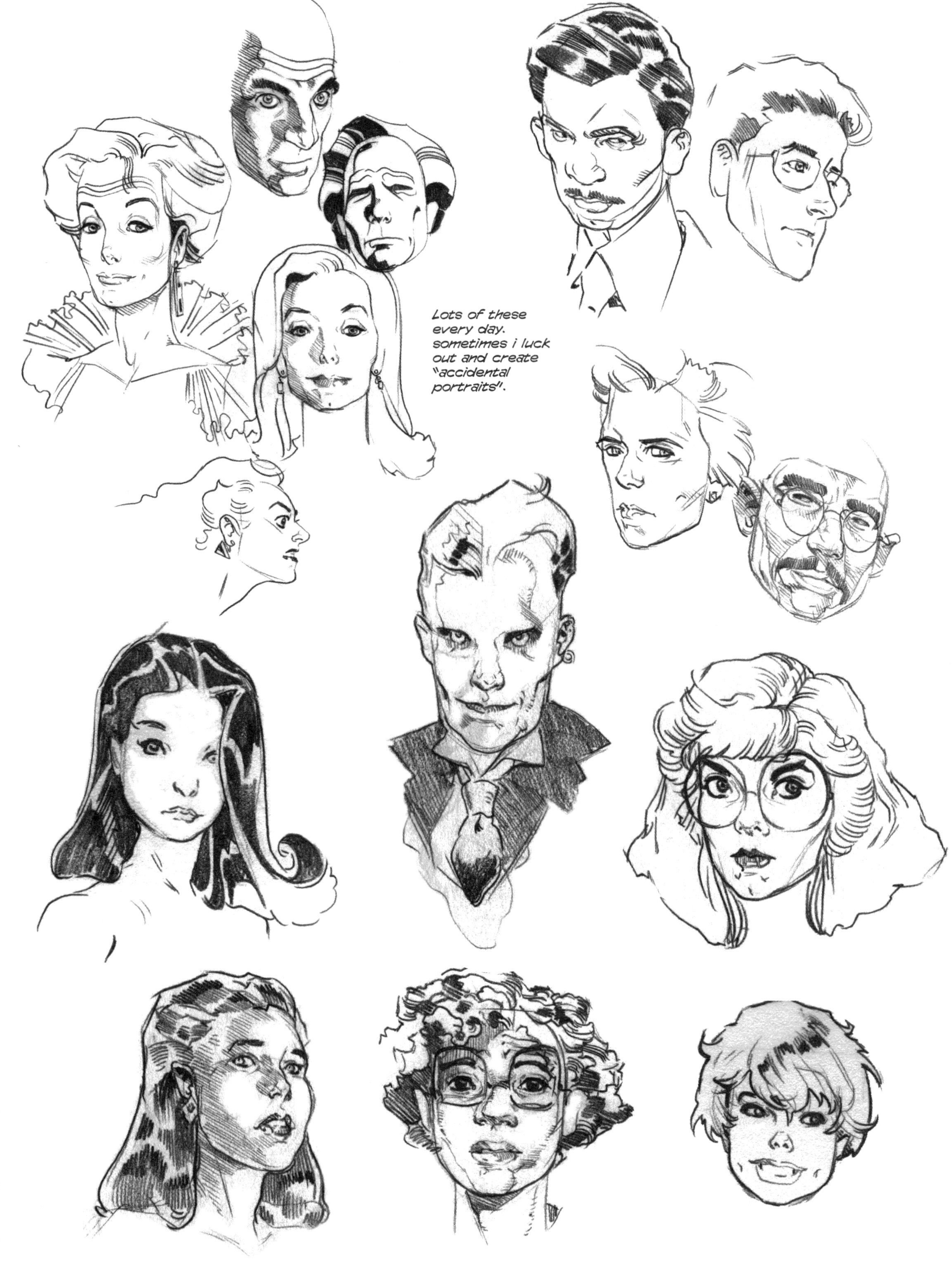
Lots of these
every day.
sometimes i luck
out and create
"accidental
portraits".

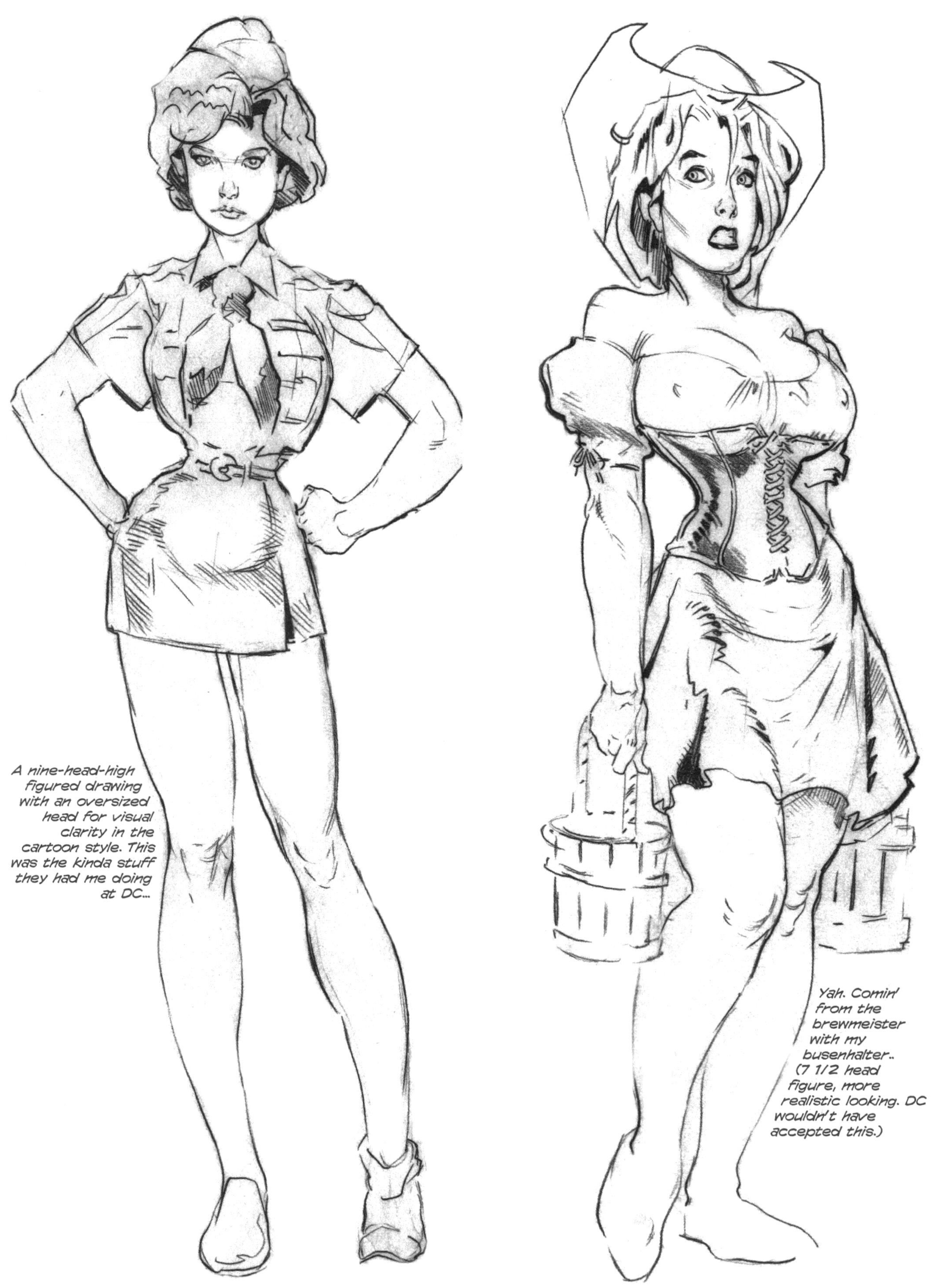

A nine-head-high figured drawing with an oversized head for visual clarity in the cartoon style. This was the kinda stuff they had me doing at DC...

Yah. Comin' from the brewmeister with my busenhalter.. (7 1/2 head figure, more realistic looking. DC wouldn't have accepted this.)

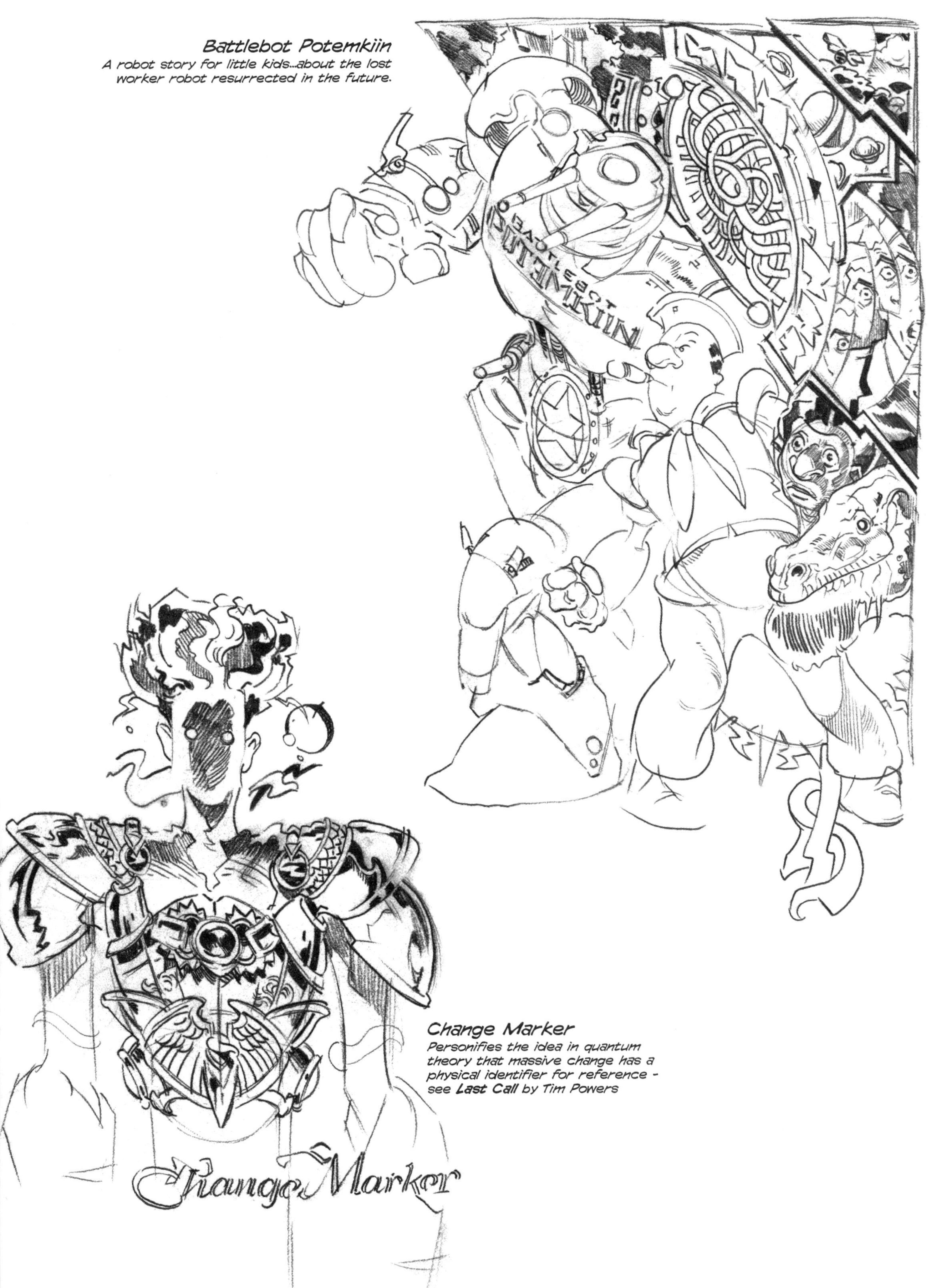

Battlebot Potemkiin

A robot story for little kids...about the lost worker robot resurrected in the future.

Change Marker

*Personifies the idea in quantum theory that massive change has a physical identifier for reference - see **Last Call** by Tim Powers*

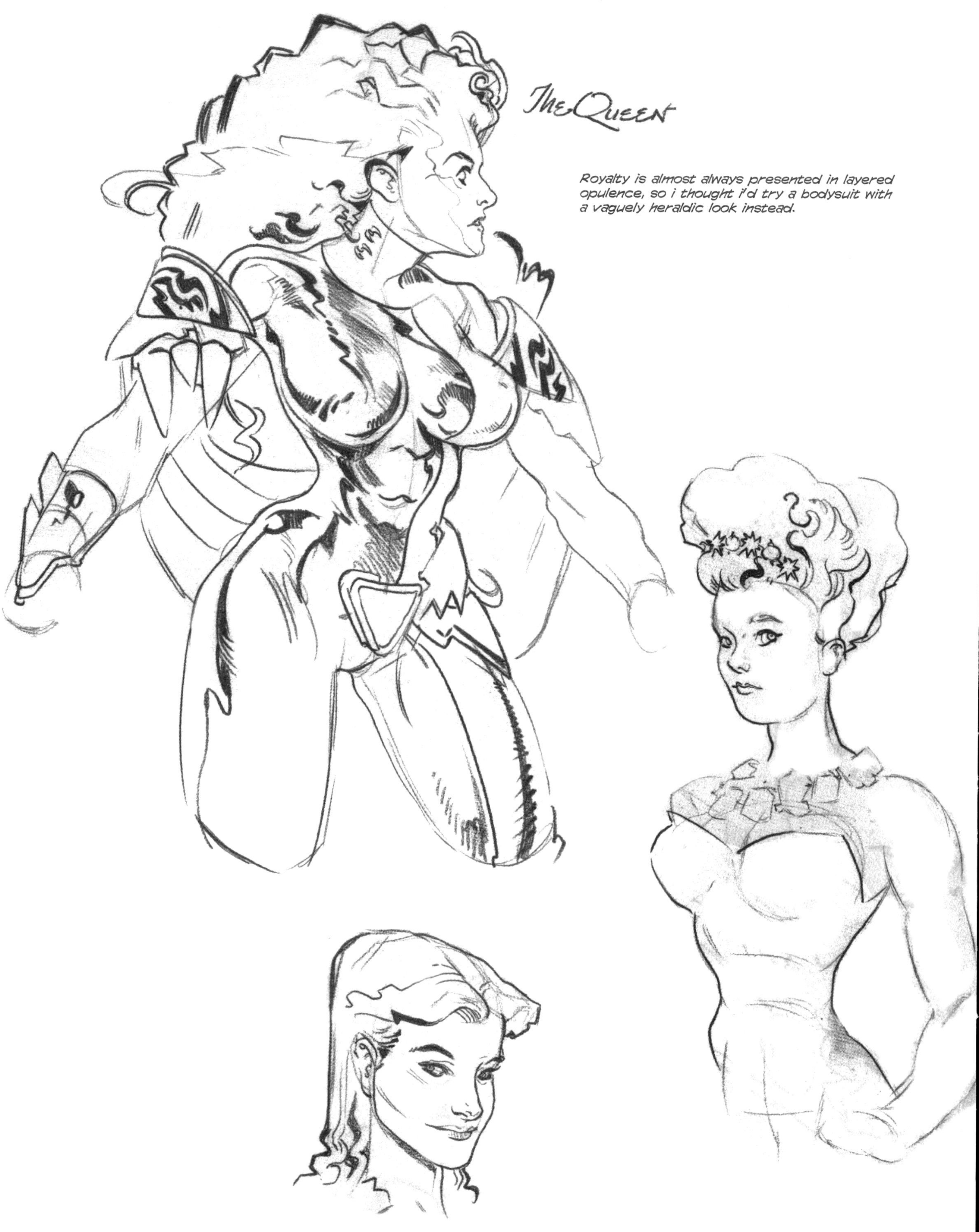
The Queen
Royalty is almost always presented in layered opulence, so i thought i'd try a bodysuit with a vaguely heraldic look instead.

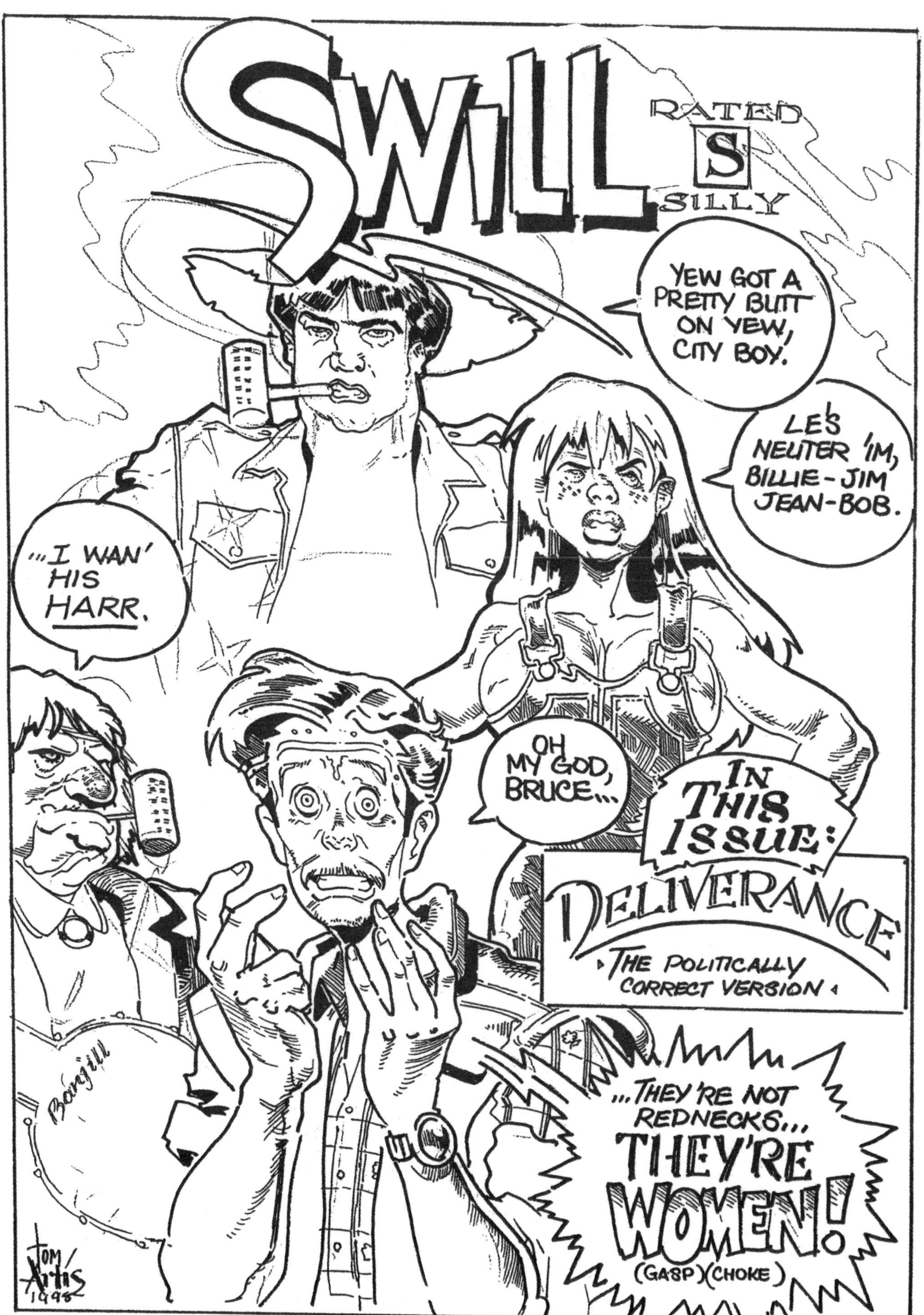

Swill 1

The concept of Swill is that everything has already been written. so the idea is to create stories based on urban legends, iconic movies, sequels you never seen, etc.

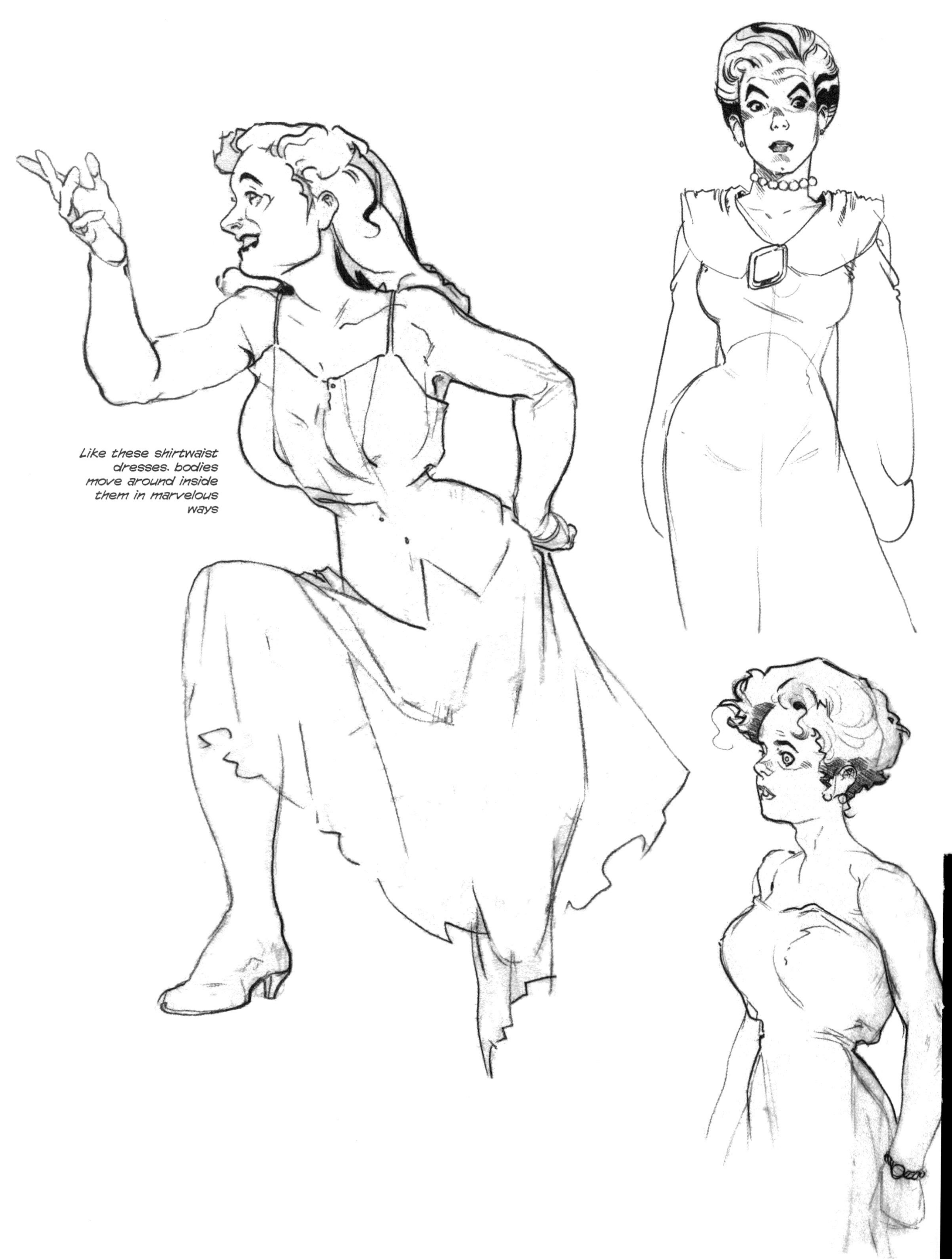

Like these shirtwaist dresses. bodies move around inside them in marvelous ways

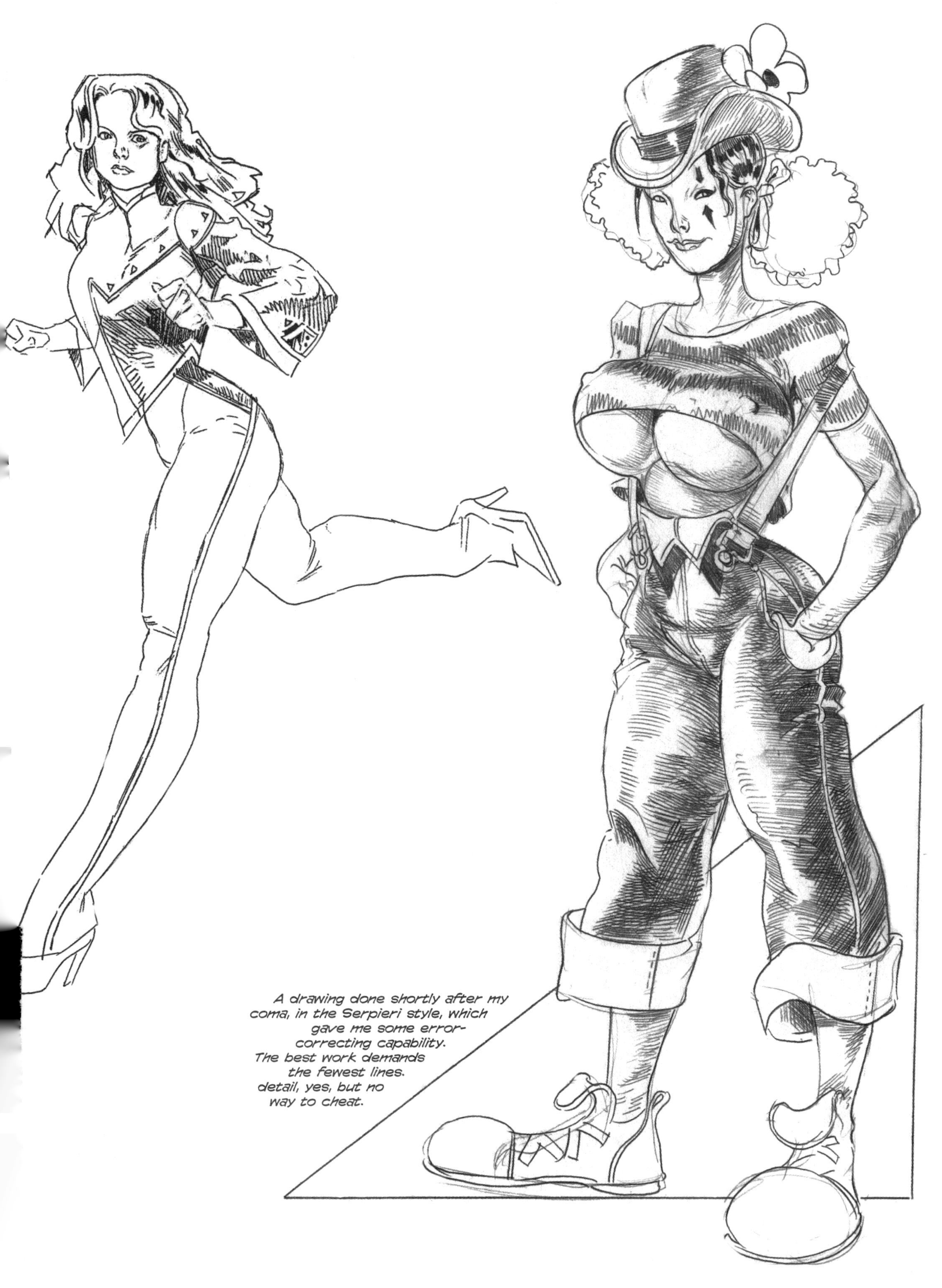

A drawing done shortly after my coma, in the Serpieri style, which gave me some error-correcting capability. The best work demands the fewest lines. detail, yes, but no way to cheat.

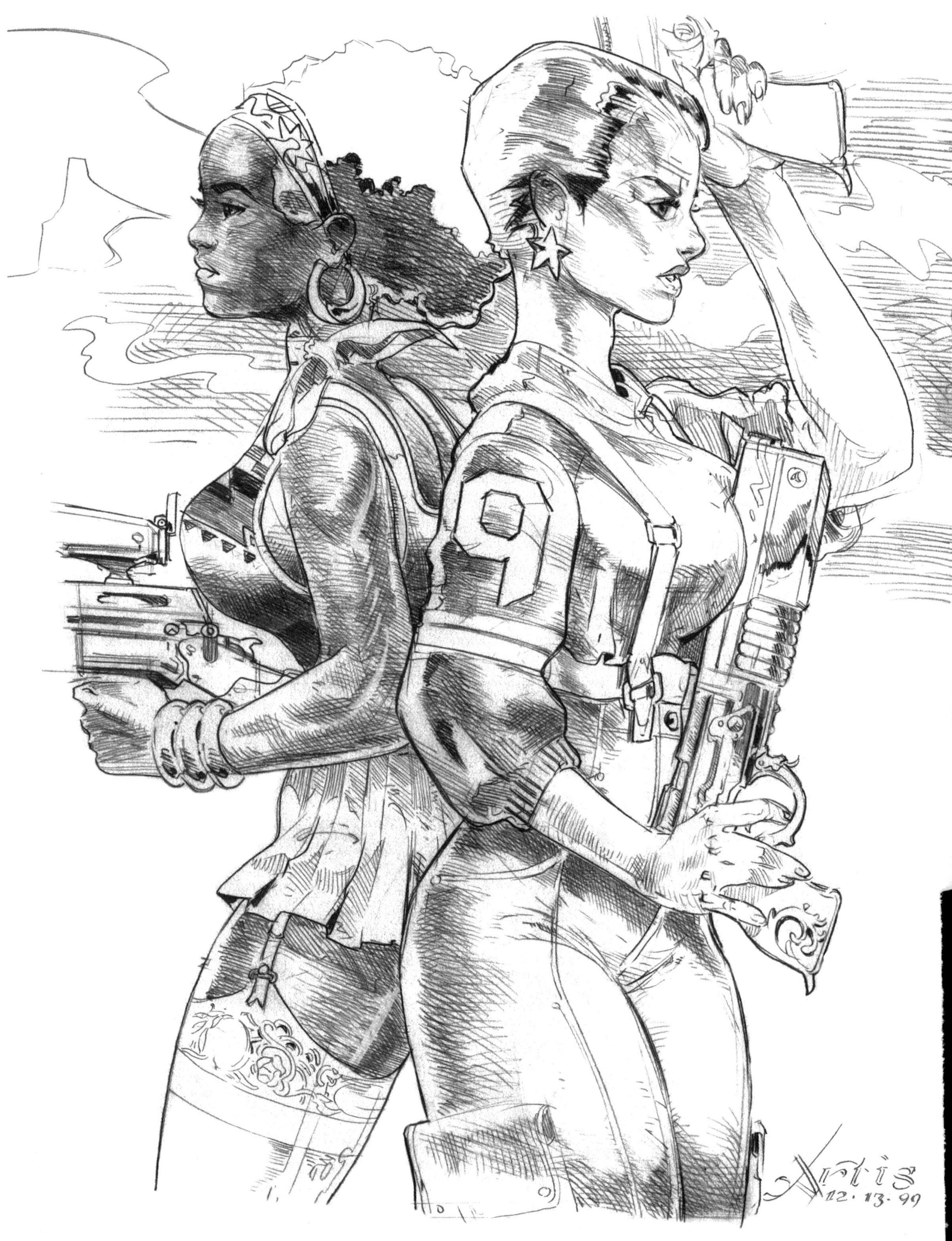
9
Artis
12.13.99